Creativity in Workforce Development and Innovation:

Emerging Research and Opportunities

Sally Blake
Flagler College, USA

Candice M. Burkett
University of Illinois at Chicago, USA

A volume in the Advances in Human Resources Management and Organizational Development (AHRMOD) Book Series

Published in the United States of America by
IGI Global
Business Science Reference (an imprint of IGI Global)
701 E. Chocolate Avenue
Hershey PA, USA 17033
Tel: 717-533-8845
Fax: 717-533-8661
E-mail: cust@igi-global.com
Web site: http://www.igi-global.com

Copyright © 2018 by IGI Global. All rights reserved. No part of this publication may be reproduced, stored or distributed in any form or by any means, electronic or mechanical, including photocopying, without written permission from the publisher.
Product or company names used in this set are for identification purposes only. Inclusion of the names of the products or companies does not indicate a claim of ownership by IGI Global of the trademark or registered trademark.

Library of Congress Cataloging-in-Publication Data

Names: Blake, Sally, 1949- author. | Burkett, Candice M., 1981- author.
Title: Creativity in workforce development and innovation : emerging research and opportunities / by Sally Blake and Candice M. Burkett.
Description: Hershey : Business Science Reference, [2017]
Identifiers: LCCN 2017032924| ISBN 9781522549529 (hardcover) | ISBN 9781522549536 (ebook)
Subjects: LCSH: Creative ability in business. | Labor supply--Effect of technological innovations on.
Classification: LCC HD53 .B5665 2017 | DDC 658.3001/9--dc23 LC record available at https://lccn.loc.gov/2017032924

This book is published in the IGI Global book series Advances in Human Resources Management and Organizational Development (AHRMOD) (ISSN: 2327-3372; eISSN: 2327-3380)

British Cataloguing in Publication Data
A Cataloguing in Publication record for this book is available from the British Library.

All work contributed to this book is new, previously-unpublished material.
The views expressed in this book are those of the authors, but not necessarily of the publisher.

For electronic access to this publication, please contact: eresources@igi-global.com.

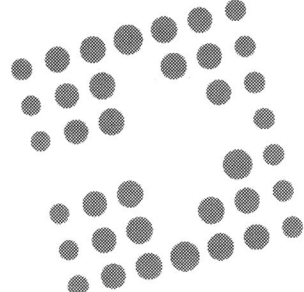

Advances in Human Resources Management and Organizational Development (AHRMOD) Book Series

ISSN:2327-3372
EISSN:2327-3380

Editor-in-Chief: Patricia Ordóñez de Pablos, Universidad de Oviedo, Spain

MISSION

A solid foundation is essential to the development and success of any organization and can be accomplished through the effective and careful management of an organization's human capital. Research in human resources management and organizational development is necessary in providing business leaders with the tools and methodologies which will assist in the development and maintenance of their organizational structure.

The **Advances in Human Resources Management and Organizational Development (AHRMOD) Book Series** aims to publish the latest research on all aspects of human resources as well as the latest methodologies, tools, and theories regarding organizational development and sustainability. The **AHRMOD Book Series** intends to provide business professionals, managers, researchers, and students with the necessary resources to effectively develop and implement organizational strategies.

COVERAGE

- Diversity in the Workplace
- Process Improvement
- Executive Education
- Personnel Policies
- Employee Benefits
- Entrepreneurialism
- Outsourcing HR
- Disputes Resolution
- Personnel Retention
- Employment and Labor Laws

IGI Global is currently accepting manuscripts for publication within this series. To submit a proposal for a volume in this series, please contact our Acquisition Editors at Acquisitions@igi-global.com or visit: http://www.igi-global.com/publish/.

The Advances in Human Resources Management and Organizational Development (AHRMOD) Book Series (ISSN 2327-3372) is published by IGI Global, 701 E. Chocolate Avenue, Hershey, PA 17033-1240, USA, www.igi-global.com. This series is composed of titles available for purchase individually; each title is edited to be contextually exclusive from any other title within the series. For pricing and ordering information please visit http://www.igi-global.com/book-series/advances-human-resources-management-organizational/73670. Postmaster: Send all address changes to above address. ©© 2018 IGI Global. All rights, including translation in other languages reserved by the publisher. No part of this series may be reproduced or used in any form or by any means – graphics, electronic, or mechanical, including photocopying, recording, taping, or information and retrieval systems – without written permission from the publisher, except for non commercial, educational use, including classroom teaching purposes. The views expressed in this series are those of the authors, but not necessarily of IGI Global.

Titles in this Series

For a list of additional titles in this series, please visit:
https://www.igi-global.com/book-series/advances-human-resources-management-organizational/73670

Evaluating Media Richness in Organizational Learning
Albert Gyamfi (Aalborg University Copenhagen, Denmark) and Idongesit Williams (Aalborg University Copenhagen, Denmark)
Business Science Reference • ©2018 • 328pp • H/C (ISBN: 9781522529569) • US $185.00

Teaching Human Resources and Organizational Behavior at the College Level
John Mendy (University of Lincoln, UK)
Business Science Reference • ©2018 • 305pp • H/C (ISBN: 9781522528203) • US $195.00

Handbook of Research on Organizational Culture and Diversity in the Modern Workforce
Bryan Christiansen (PryMarke LLC, USA) and Harish C. Chandan (Argosy University, USA)
Business Science Reference • ©2017 • 506pp • H/C (ISBN: 9781522522508) • US $255.00

Handbook of Research on Human Factors in Contemporary Workforce Development
Bryan Christiansen (PryMarke LLC, USA) and Harish C. Chandan (Argosy University, USA)
Business Science Reference • ©2017 • 563pp • H/C (ISBN: 9781522525684) • US $255.00

Driving Multinational Enterprises Through Effective Global Talent Management
Khaled Tamzini (University of Sousse, Tunisia) Tahar Lazhar Ayed (Umm Al-Qura University, Saudi Arabia) Aisha Wood Boulanouar (Sultan Qaboos University, Muscat, Oman) and Zakaria Boulanouar (Umm Al-Qura University, Saudi Arabia)
Business Science Reference • ©2017 • 191pp • H/C (ISBN: 9781522525578) • US $170.00

Exploring the Influence of Personal Values and Cultures in the Workplace
Zlatko Nedelko (University of Maribor, Slovenia) and Maciej Brzozowski (Poznan University of Economics and Business, Poland)
Business Science Reference • ©2017 • 458pp • H/C (ISBN: 9781522524809) • US $205.00

Effective Talent Management Strategies for Organizational Success
Mambo Mupepi (Grand Valley State University, USA)
Business Science Reference • ©2017 • 365pp • H/C (ISBN: 9781522519614) • US $210.00

For an enitre list of titles in this series, please visit:
https://www.igi-global.com/book-series/advances-human-resources-management-organizational/73670

701 East Chocolate Avenue, Hershey, PA 17033, USA
Tel: 717-533-8845 x100 • Fax: 717-533-8661
E-Mail: cust@igi-global.com • www.igi-global.com

Table of Contents

Foreword vi

Preface ix

Chapter 1
The Case for Creativity and Innovation 1

Chapter 2
What Is Creativity? 23

Chapter 3
What Stops Creativity? 46

Chapter 4
The Science of Creativity 67

Chapter 5
Individual Creativity: Predictors and Characteristics 88

Chapter 6
Creative Transformation: Setting the Stage for Workplace Creativity and Innovation 105

Related Readings 129

About the Authors 150

Index 151

Foreword

Creativity is about survival. In ancient civilizations, people used what was available to them in resourceful ways to meet the challenges they faced. In the history of the United States, there has been an impressive array of constructive enterprises in which ingenuity, or creativity, has resulted in a better quality of life for the nation. On a more practical level, creativity is customary in our everyday lives. On a regular basis, adults devise artful approaches for integrating their multiple roles as parents, spouses, workers, caretakers, volunteers, friends, and lifelong learners. Likewise, teenagers arrange functional schedules that allow them to carve out time for multiple homework assignments, sports participation, part-time employment, community service, household chores, social networking, and leisure pursuits. I am certain that many individuals would not consider these daily balancing acts examples of creativity. Not only would I beg to differ, but also, I would encourage them to consider viewing creativity through a different, more expansive lens.

Chase Jarvis, co-founder of CreativeLive, an online education platform designed to promote creative education, has characterized creativity as the new literacy. In one fundamental way, this comparison is an apt analogy. For decades, professionals struggled to come to consensus on a single definition for literacy. However, these debates attenuated as a reasonable conclusion was reached: that literacy is not a single construct. Rather, the concept of literacy could subsume a variety of domains including print, visual, digital, media, information, and cultural literacy. Similarly, creativity can be viewed as being multifaceted. Its various facets have come into sharper focus as it is being increasingly viewed as extending beyond the province of the arts. In Bloom's Revised Taxonomy, the change in terminology from *synthesis* to *create* as the highest level of cognitive processing has helped to broaden the traditional arts-only conceptualization of creativity to encompass any endeavor that involves the combination of elements into a cohesive, operative whole and organizing—or reorganizing—elements into innovative structures and

Foreword

products. This envisioning of the creative process has resulted in a paradigm shift that allows for the appreciation of the creativity evident in not only an evocative painting or a decorative ceramic bowl, but also the artistry reflected in an insightful strategic plan, a flourishing business, an engaging lesson, a salubrious massage, an original recipe, or a workable agenda of daily activities.

It is these frequently unrecognized versions of creativity that promote the type of productivity that contributes to successful outcomes in a society, because effective strategies are, necessarily, temporary approaches and, therefore, must change perpetually to accommodate the fact that perspectives, individuals, communities, and nations continually evolve. In reality, astute employers are always divining the employment landscape to determine anticipated job content and positions in order to remain relevant and robust. By extension, curriculum developers for schools, the major suppliers of human resources for the workplace, are always in the predictive mode of formulating standards that prepare students for many jobs that do not yet exist. At best, present and future workers are optimally prepared for the vagaries of an advancing society by providing them with multiple opportunities to be creative—that is, to synthesize their present repertoire of knowledge and skills in flexible ways to fulfill the singular requirements that a particular task or responsibility demands.

It must be noted, however, that creativity cannot thrive in an atmosphere of resistance and rigid adherence to the status quo and the way things were. CEOs, managers, administrators, teachers, and others in influential positions must be willing to transcend the one-right-answer, one-size-fits-all mentality and become more receptive to affirming multiple pathways to progress and achievement. Often, this unwillingness does not derive from a penchant for inertia, but rather from a necessity for principles, strategies, and tools to foster creativity in a way that maximizes the level of critical thinking, problem solving, and inventiveness that can sustain a vibrant and dynamic workplace. This book can be enormously helpful in meeting that need.

The aim of this book is to contribute to a greater understanding of creativity and to emphasize its importance as a human resource asset in the workplace. It includes a wealth of content that comprehensively examines the dimensions of creativity in multiple contexts that will, no doubt, enlighten readers who may acquire the book for a variety of purposes. Even more important, in addition to information and research on creativity, it contains ideas and applications that are translatable into practice and can support workplace leaders in their efforts to promote and harness creative potential that will equip the workforce with the enhanced capacity to approach tasks and discharge responsibilities in innovative ways that will increase the viability of businesses and industries in a competitive, complex, and changing world.

Carl Williams
Flagler College, USA

Carl Williams *is one of Flagler's most distinguished professors in the education department at Flagler College. The Schultz Grant recipient and widely published professor has been honored with the Dean's Award for Excellence in Professional Development, the Outstanding Professor of the Year Award and the SGA Faculty Member of the Year Award. Williams received his Ed.D. in educational leadership and his M.Ed. in special education from the University of North Florida; he received his B.A. in deaf education and English from Flagler College. He teaches several courses in deaf education at Flagler and serves as the Secondary English Education Coordinator. Prior to his service at Flagler, Williams taught at the Florida School for the Deaf and Blind. His innovation in instruction and dedication to deaf education led to the 2006 publication of his text "It All Depends, A Casebook for Prospective Teachers of Students Who are Deaf and Hard of Hearing," a case study book in deaf education. His reviews heralded his innovation and creative approach to work with this population. Williams is also the author of "No Limits: A practical guide for teaching deaf and hard of hearing students," which broke ground in deaf education as the first book of its kind to correlate with the Council on Educating the Deaf standards and the Educational Content Standards in Deaf Education. Williams is a sought-after presenter on issues in deaf education. To view his discussion of "No Limits," visit https://vimeo.com/11325391.*

Preface

There are many reasons why creativity is here to stay, rather than a trendy buzzword or passing phase. Benefits of investing in innovation and creativity include greater national competitiveness and higher income levels (McCarthy, 2016). The generation of new and valuable ideas is a core component in the ability of individuals and groups both to respond adaptively to change and to envision and bring about change (Runco, 2006). As such, creativity is of central importance to human, social, and economic development.

A 2014 study from Adobe Systems Incorporated found a high percentage of agreement across counties that creativity drives economic growth. Creativity and entrepreneurial thinking is a skill set highly associated with job creation, critical thinking and problem-solving skills (Pink, 2005; Robinson, 2006; Sternberg & Lubart, 1996). Hanushek, Jamison, Jamison, Eliot, and Woessmann (2008) identify these as "cognitive skills," and believe they differentiate the economic leaders from the laggards among 50 countries from 1960 to 2000. Among other benefits, a highly skilled work force can raise economic growth by about two-thirds of a percentage point every year. Worldwide, the average annual Gross Domestic Product (GDP) growth rate for more than half a century is 2 to 3 percent, so this is a significant boost. Those countries that produce the most important new products and services can capture a premium in world markets that will enable them to pay high wages to their citizens (National Center on Education and the Economy, 2007).

The book is important for the field of education and business; however, it also contributes to theory and practice of creativity and innovation across multiple domains. The book discusses in detail the importance of creativity, what creativity is, how it emerges in educational and organizational settings and what supports creativity. A reviewer wrote that to date, there has not been a book written on the topic that analyzes so many facets of creativity and from so many perspectives. The book should appeal to management (for effective ways to foster creativity) and employees who fear they cannot be creative.

Preface

This work started as an investigation into the declining creativity in educational systems and what teacher preparation programs were doing to support this critical attribute. It has evolved into a much larger study on why creativity is so important to the global workplace and workforce. The authors were identified as highly creative at young ages and have survived the education and work environments that rarely valued characteristics of creative people. In the new global society creativity is valued in the workplace and has become a new standard for success. Some consider creativity the new literacy. This book provides information about the importance of creativity in this era of growing complexity and rapid change, provides research about creativity and recommendations for development and sustainability.

The authors aim to present ideas that support the potential of the democratic creativity view which differs from the elite perception of creative individuals. Within us all sleeps the potential for creative thinking yet something stops or inhibits this development. Complacency is no longer an option in the creative age: developing, supporting and sustaining the creative potential of all individuals is the blueprint for the future of the workplace.

The books starts with the justification for creativity in the workplace and across work and education domains. Next the many definitions of creativity are explored and myths about creative thinking and individuals are busted. Each chapter includes a quote for reflection from Steve Jobs, the renowned master of identifying creativity and turning this into innovation. His work inspired the development of creative worksites and the importance of allowing workers to collaborate and create, not just obey. The next two chapters explore the research on how the functions of the brain connect to creativity. The last chapter addresses elements of creative change to transform the workplace into a more productive environment.

In Chapter 1, the authors build a case for creativity. Some consider the workplace focus on creativity as a passing phase, soon to be discarded like other trends of the past. The chapter explores the changes in the global workforce and how the expectations for the new work skills support creativity and innovation. Many of the fastest-growing jobs and emerging industries rely on workers' creative capacity—the ability to think unconventionally, question the herd, imagine new scenarios and produce astonishing work (National Academies of Science, 2016). Support for creativity comes from economics, business, health care and education systems and the demand will increase not diminish and disappear. In this evolving environment, creative workers will not just survive but will thrive, secure in their future roles as drivers, not spare tires to the norm. Innovation is here and the time to celebrate has arrived for creative thinkers across all levels of the workforce.

Preface

Chapter 2 addresses the elusive definition of creativity and the many research studies about this construct. The authors propose that creativity is possible in all people, not just an elite few. Everyone has creative thoughts; however, it is the application of these thoughts that produces innovated approaches to problems or the vision of the needs of the future workforce. A model of the relationship of creativity and innovation can be found in this chapter which illustrates connections to imagination. An interesting section of chapter two challenges the myths and misconceptions that are prevalent about creativity and creative people. It may be a surprise to read about how creative thinking and creative personalities are perceived as these ideas can marginalize employment opportunities. A subsection of myths and misconceptions includes common beliefs concerning structure of the finance and high-tech industries' workplace which are actually the antithesis of creative thinking and productivity.

Perhaps the greatest concern, educational environments, is discussed in Chapter 3. Educational systems influence creativity and innovation through environments, socialization, and reward systems. Schools are practice for the workplace and set the stage for beliefs about how learning should occur. What happens there is repeated for years to socialize the future workforce on what acceptable interactions and thinking are which influences what happens in our worksites. Schools are the first place children share their creative thinking outside of their home environment. Studies indicate that the longer a student stays in the school system the lower their ability to think creatively becomes.

Another confounding variable comes from the research about how teachers perceive creative children. There is some evidence to support teachers do not like creative thinking and they identify "ideal" students as those who behave and do not question the status quo. Teachers favor children with the least creative traits. Our school systems make creativity the nearly exclusive property of antisocial personality types (Epstein, 1999).

Admission requirements for many teacher preparation programs ignore creativity and use traditional tests like ACT and SAT. One study found that the lower the creativity level the higher the ACT score. This is a major concern as we continue to send these graduates into schools already following a factory model of education to prepare a generation where creativity will determine success of the workforce. This conflicting paradigm of demands for success in the global community and the measures of academic achievement in many schools seems counterproductive, at best, for the millions of students coming through the educational systems.

Chapter 4 discusses evidence to support that all individuals have creative potential through a review of the relevant neurological and cognitive literatures which suggests that creative thinking is rooted in everyday cognitive mechanisms and processes. This chapter explores what conclusions can be drawn from neuroscience and cognitive studies about the creative brain. There is no doubt that creativity is dependent on processes and connections generated in the brain. The question is- what brain processes are most related to creative thought and where in the brain do those processes take place? There is a great deal of evidence to support that there is a relationship between various aspects of executive functioning and creativity. Some researchers subscribe to the notion that creative thought actually includes some processes that would benefit from reduced inhibition and some processes that would benefit from greater inhibitory control. The fact that creativity is rooted in everyday mental processes is promising for the presence of creativity in the workplace. If, in fact, creativity is not some elusive gene that belongs only to the chosen few- then it can be fostered and nurtured both by individual practices as well as elements of the environment. The implication of findings as those descried in this chapter is that we are all equipped with a brain that is complex enough for us to think creatively. In other words, we all have the potential to be creative. Although some realize that potential more fully than others, the necessary elements to support creative thinking are present in all of us.

Chapter 5 builds on Chapter 4 to discuss how individual creativity connects to the psychological constructs of intelligence, personality, intrinsic motivation, and to provide readers with some identifying behaviors of creative people. It is important to note, however, that having the potential to be engaged in creative thought does not automatically mean that one will do so.

As the study of creativity has expanded to include brain neurology; however, some scientists question whether any standard definition or tests for it still make sense. It is perhaps best thought of as a process, requiring a mixture of ingredients, including personality traits, abilities, and skills (Kounios et al., 2006; Kounios, 2010). This is supported by a creativity inventory list included in this chapter to help identify clusters of behaviors exhibited by creative individuals.

Creative people actively seek new solutions to problems, are comfortable with ambiguity, curious, willing to communicate creative thinking, serve as models for professional development of other workers, and look beyond

Preface

information to find connections. Consequently, identifying creative applicants or existing employees can help leaders plan and develop an intentional working climate built on individual creative potential in any profession which supports a culture of creativity. There are also recommendations for formal inventories to identify creativity levels in individuals. The leader is tasked to plan ways to build on individual creativity and support efforts to change the traditional workplace into an innovation generator propelled by creativity. Identifying and connecting the strengths of a diverse workforce is challenging but necessary.

Chapter 6 provides ideas for creative transformation across influencing categories associated with the workplace of the future. Managing any workplace is a delicate balance. The issue is keeping the workflow moving forward while providing an environment that encourages creativity and innovation. In order to stimulate creativity, employers must first create a great work place environment where employees are encouraged to contribute. No change is easy but by reinventing the corporate culture and the office environment to place more emphasis on creativity, organizations are reaping the benefits and becoming leaders in their respective industries (Genever, 2016). One aspect that seems tied to the new generation of workers deals with the psychosocial aspect of the workplace. The new generation of workers are well accustomed to social communication and spend a lot of time using electronic devices. It is a part of their culture and finding ways to incorporate this into the workplace is important. The workplace has become an important social support environment in the creativity age. This has brought attention to the emotional expectations of the new breed of workers which is almost a direct opposite of the traditional thinking about interactions in the working environment. The new employees expect managers to address their emotional needs, rather a tough situation for those trained to ignore such things. This chapter offers ideas for creative transformation to the new needs of this generation of workers. It is time for a new era in the workplace—an era of creativity that will redefine how organizations function.

The authors hope that those who read this book will think about the workplace in a different manner than generations before. It is also hoped that educators will reflect on how students are socialized in educational environments and develop new approaches to teacher preparation admissions requirements and teacher training.

REFERENCES

Epstein, R. (1999). Generativity Theory. In M. A. Runco & S. Pritzker (Eds.), Encyclopedia of Creativity (pp. 759–766). Academic Press.

Genever, H. (2016). 4 ways to cultivate workplace creativity. *Lifeplan.* Retrieved from https://www.liveplan.com/blog/2016/06/4-ways-to-cultivate-workplace-creativity-a-liveplan-guide/

Kounios, J. (2010, May 8). Charting creativity: Signposts of a hazy territory. *New York Times*, p. C1.

Kounios, J., Frymiare, J. L., Bowden, E. M., Fleck, J. I., Subramaniam, K., Parrish, T. B., & Jung-Beeman, M. J. (2006). The prepared mind: Neural activity prior to problem presentation predicts subsequent solution by sudden insight. *Psychological Science, 17*(10), 882–890. doi:10.1111/j.1467-9280.2006.01798.x PMID:17100789

McCarthy, N. (2016). *The world's most creative cities.* Retrieved from https://www.statista.com/chart/6578/the-worlds-most-creative-cities/

National Academies of Sciences, Engineering, and Medicine (NASEM). (2016). *Developing a National STEM Workforce Strategy: A Workshop Summary.* Washington, DC: The National Academies Press. doi: 10.17226/21900

National Center on Education and the Economy. (2007). *Tough choices or tough times: The report of the new commission on the skills of the American workforce.* Washington, DC: Author.

Pink, D. H. (2005). *A whole new mind: Why right-brainers will rule the Future.* New York: Riverhead Hardcover.

Robinson, K. (1999). *All our futures: Creativity, culture and education. A report to the Department of Education and Employment, Department for Culture, Media and Sport.* London: Department of Education and Employment.

Runco, M. A. (2006). The development of children's creativity. In B. Spodek & N. Saracho (Eds.), *Handbook of the research on the education of young children* (pp. 121–131). Mahwah, NJ: Erlbaum.

Sternberg, R. J., & Lubart, T. I. (1996). Investing in creativity. *The American Psychologist, 51*(7), 677–688. doi:10.1037/0003-066X.51.7.677

Chapter 1
The Case for Creativity and Innovation

ABSTRACT

The world has moved on and away from the traditional work environment. The workforce characteristics have changed, as have expectations of the working population and the workplace. Jobs that did not exist ten years ago, are accepted and new positions continue to develop globally as science and communication systems change. Changes in expectations for a global workforce continue to gain support across disciplines as skills needed to solve problems creatively become necessary to react and develop solutions to unpredictable and inherent risks. Today's society demands creative and novel resolutions, valuable ideas, as well as adaptation and vision to bring about change. Inspiring, sustaining and applying creativity is necessary to compete in today's breathlessly evolving marketplace. The purpose of this chapter is to provide a case for the importance of creativity in the workplace.

INTRODUCTION: TO CREATE OR NOT TO CREATE

Some would argue that creativity has become a buzzword, implying that it is fashionable at this time in context- simply a passing phase or trend. Runco and Jaeger (2012) write that creativity has value depending on the current market; however, the authors believe that creativity is essential for the *future* of business, health services, general education and the global workforce. Rather than thinking of creativity as the outcome of a series of processes,

DOI: 10.4018/978-1-5225-4952-9.ch001

the adaptation of "older" ideas to generate applications to the new world of technology and global systems is, in itself, a creative thinking process. The authors propose that creativity and innovation in this era should be valued more as a worldview, or a critical thinking process, rather than just an end product. This view suggests that creativity is particularly important to problem solving- as leaders, managers and workers alike further develop their abilities to switch strategies if they find that a solution is not forthcoming. The new world of workers must constantly evaluate information, including the discrimination of relevant from irrelevant information, which influence successful choices for and approaches to managing issues across various domains (Johnston & Bate, 2013). From these important thinking processes, innovation grows through application. Limiting thinking concerning the importance of creativity to *all* aspects of professional endeavors is, in itself, inhibiting the development and support of this critical attribute.

Objectives

In this chapter the authors will explore the changes in the global workforce and how the expectations for the new work skills support creativity and innovation. The chapter includes summary information across disciplines to include research reports, CEO blog sites, and recommendations from agencies like the National Academies of Science and The Partnership for 21st Century Skills. The scope of identified need for both creativity and innovation indicate this is not the "pet rock" of our era, but necessary to transcend political borders and improve the quality of life as well as economic success from a global perspective.

After reading this chapter one should be able to identify the support for creativity as a constant and necessary component of the changing expectations for the workforce and workplace. The reader should develop a better understanding of the shift in the working population and, therefore, the demand for creativity across multiple industries.

BACKGROUND: THE CHANGING WORKFORCE

If you're gonna make connections which are innovative ... you have to not have the same bag of experiences as everyone else does. - Steve Jobs (1982)

It's Not Your Father's Workforce Anymore

What do these terms have in common: YouTube Sex Ed Teacher, Simulated Astronaut, Vegan Butcher, Professional Activist, Bug Bounty Hunter, Death Doula, and Compost Collector? According to the January 25 issue of Time Magazine these are seven new jobs created in 2017. For many years jobs have pretty much stayed the same with some variation on the tools and skills needed for job performance. However, as technology use has increased the world of employment has drastically changed. Technology has introduced new flexibility to both employers and employees alike, allowing employees in some positions a greater sense of freedom, employers a higher degree of efficiency, and greater connectedness for both without the traditional limitations of time and place (ADP, 2016b). Simultaneously many other population factors are changing including age, gender, diversity, education and skills, as well as increase in demand for temporary and freelance workers (Vander Ark, 2012). Previously, individuals defined security by tenure, or length of stay. Today, with shifts in the workplace, employees define security by the reach of their professional network and the ability to tap into relationships to find non-linear jobs that can extend a career (SHRM Foundation, 2015). Employees' demand for greater choice and flexibility, access to real-time learning, increased autonomy, a sense of stability, and the ability to work on personally meaningful projects are driving global workplace transformation (ADP, 2016a).

Population Factors

Four population factors are greatly influencing the makeup of the current and future workforce profile including age, gender, education, skills, and increases in temporary and freelance workers. These factors impact not only the makeup of the work*force*, but also the environment of the work*place*. In fact, these factors, which are further compounded by technology, have changed the very worldview of work.

Age

Aging is currently considered the most significant macro trend causing the workforce of the future to look significantly different from the workforce represented in current practices, policies and law (International Labor

Organization, 2013). The traditional definition of the working-age population, usually defined as those aged 15-64, has been shifting slowly over time. First, workers are staying in the workforce longer. The Bureau of Labor Statistics in the United States predicts that 35 percent of men aged 65-74 will be in the workforce by 2020, up from 25 percent in 2000 (Stanford Center on Longevity, 2013). Second, younger workers are searching for meaning beyond lucrative salaries in order to feel fulfilled. In the 2016 ADP survey of the Changing Workforce of 2000 working age from thirteen countries 89 percent of respondents indicated they will choose to work on personal interests/things that impact society and 82 percent will define their own work schedule (ADP Research Institute, 2016a). Third, the once rapid increase in the participation rate (either already employed or actively seeking employment) of the youth labor force (aged 15-24) is now beginning to shrink. The youth labor force participation rate has been falling for some time now, as more young people leave the workforce to continue their education or because they are discouraged from looking for work after long-term unemployment. This transformation of the age structure of the population will have a profound impact on the make-up of the workforce globally. Pronounced variations exist across countries with regard to the ageing of their populations and the size of their youth labor force. However, the influence of age variables and the workforce trend of change is evident globally.

Gender

A little over half of the world's population is composed of women, yet their contribution to economic activity and growth remains below its full potential. Women have become an increasingly well-educated source of talent, outnumbering men in tertiary education at a rate of 108 to 100 in 2012 globally. Gender equality is considered a core development objective and is integral to economic growth, business growth and good development outcomes (World Bank, 2015). However, women are still disproportionately represented in low-skilled fields and vulnerable employment opportunities, which has contributed to a significant gender wage differential. This is particularly true in societies with traditional views of gender roles, where women account for a much larger share of the unpaid labor force, of the informal sector (jobs that are often low-paid, temporary and exempt from taxes and other government regulations), and of the poor (SHRM Foundation, 2015). Through education and access to the formal economy, empowering women can sharply increase the global human potential to address societal challenges. Highly regarded development programs focus on this gender potential across all sectors, given the power of science, technology, and innovation to contribute to the advancement of women. Expanding women's opportunities leads to better living conditions (NASEM, 2017a).

Education and Skills

Globally, the workforce is becoming more "skilled" and specialized. During the period 1990-2010 the gross enrolment ratio in tertiary education over the world more than doubled from 13.6 percent to 29.2 percent (SHRM Foundation, 2015). There are still disparities among countries with regard to educational attainment, but also with regard to the quality of education and skills attained. The OECD launched a survey in 2012, the Program for the International Assessment of Adult Competencies (PIAAC), across 22 OECD countries to measure levels of literacy, numeracy (or mathematical literacy) and problem-solving among adults in the workplace (OECD, 2013). The study found that almost one-third of adults in Italy, Spain and the U.S. performed poorly in numeracy, compared with only one in eight in Finland and the Czech Republic and less than one in ten in Japan. Countries with greater socioeconomic inequality overall fared more poorly than those with more egalitarian societies, such as the Nordic countries (The Economist, 2013). South Korea's older workers ranked poorly, but the younger workers massively outperformed them, which is attributed to rigorous school reforms, which yield relatively quick results.

Temporary and Freelance Workers

Temporary workers, employees who are contracted to work for a short period of time either directly through a company or through a recruitment agency, include temporary migration workers—workers who move to a host country temporarily—and temporary workers who either work remotely or are hired locally for a short term to meet immediate demand or to provide specialization. In the past, organizations fostered a corporate culture as a fundamental element which ensures that the employees of an organization remain engaged and connected. In 2004, George P Huber, in his book *The Necessary Nature of Future Firms: Attributes of Survivors in a Changing World*, suggests that the use of temporary workers, especially those who work remotely, weakens a firm's culture. This view is no longer appropriate for the new workforce who will be more mobile. It is predicated that 4 in 10 workers will be freelancers or temporary workers (Vander Ark, 2012). In addition, these workers will hold multiple jobs at the same time. The economic implications of this more flexible workforce are significant. Workers can pursue more meaningfully independent lives. Businesses can access the exact right skills and people they need at the exact right time. A nimbler economy is potentially more innovative, more competitive, and better able to deal with the fluctuations of global markets (Freelancers Union, n.d.).

The profile of the future global worker entails a myriad of characteristics (SHRM Foundation, 2015):

- An older, more gender and ethnically diverse workforce, with increased interconnectivity, will be the standard;
- Country of origin and ethnicity no longer dictate a worker's geographical scope, especially with develop*ing* countries producing at least as many skilled, educated workers and managers as develop*ed* countries;
- Working from remote locations no longer prevents employees from communicating with their colleagues, allowing teams to collaborate with ease across national borders and time zones;
- Increased global connectivity means that workers can move around more frequently and might choose to migrate for both permanent and temporary jobs.

At the same time the workforce population is changing, the skills needed for success in the workplace are also changing. Finding and supporting the connections between these two variables for successful economic, sociocultural change is the challenge. The world has moved on. This simple but powerful phrase associated with Stephen King's Dark Tower series (1982) communicates that the world, as we have known it, no longer exists. This is the case for the changing face of the global jobs and workforce. However, unlike the gunslinger's world in the famous series, changes in the global job market does not mark the end, but, rather, the beginning of new opportunities and innovative approaches to the economic, business, health care and education systems. As the workforce becomes global due to economic, political, social and technological changes, the dynamics have been altered extensively (SHRM Foundation, 2015). If we continue to live with solutions to the past, we cannot prepare for the future.

CHANGES IN EXPECTATIONS OF THE GLOBAL WORKFORCE: CREATE BEFORE IT IS TOO LATE

The evidence for the changing expectations of the global workforce comes from a variety of sources across disciplines. In this section the authors will include information that supports the need for increased creativity and innovation. Many of the fastest-growing jobs and emerging industries rely on workers' creative capacity—the ability to think unconventionally, question the herd, imagine new scenarios and produce astonishing work (NASEM, 2016a). The best employers the world over will be looking for the most competent, most creative, and most innovative people on the face of the earth and will be willing to pay them top dollar for their services. This will be true not just for top professionals and managers, but up and down the length and breadth of the workforce (NASEM, 2016b).

Creativity is an essential connection to social foundations and cultural traditions as social relevant points are challenged in the face of rapid and constant changes (OECD, 2013; Cheng, Burks, Lee, 2009; Chuang, 2013; Rietzschel & Caniels, 2013; Runco, Lubart, & Getz, 2012). Without creative individuals, we would not be able to enjoy the innovation that punctuates our lives on a daily basis (Rabotapi, 2012). However, creativity is far more than merely a social or cultural support. More than a decade ago Florida (2006) identified the age we were entering as the creative age because the key factor propelling us forward is the rise of creativity as the primary mover of our economy. Changes in expectations for a global workforce continue to gain support across disciplines as skills needed to solve problems creatively become necessary to react and develop solutions to unpredictable and inherent risks. These changes affect both the way employees engage with one another and the tools they use to get their jobs done. While these shifts may vary across geographic location, industry, or position, there is no doubt that employers and employees must adapt as quickly as these changes are taking place (ADP, 2016b).

Benefits of Creativity

There are many reasons why creativity is here to stay, rather than a trendy buzzword or passing phase. Benefits of investing in innovation and creativity include greater national competitiveness and higher income levels (McCarthy, 2016). The generation of new and valuable ideas is a core component in the ability of individuals and groups both to respond adaptively to change and to envision and bring about change (Runco, 2006). As such, creativity is of central importance to human, social, and economic development (Johnston & Bate, 2013).

An IBM poll of 1,500 chief executive officers identified creativity as the number one "leadership competency" of the future, (Bronson & Merryman, 2010). By giving individuals the opportunity to showcase their creativity within a broad range of disciplines, both organizations and educational bodies alike would be meaningfully contributing towards the creation of fresh innovation on a broad scale (Robinson, 1999).

Creative Problem Solving is generally considered a requirement for present and future success (Runco, Lubart, & Getz, 2012). Creative skills needed to engage in creative problem solving have more easily observed effects on the cognitive than on the emotional dimensions (Runco, Lubart, & Getz, 2012). This indicates that creative behaviors can not only be quantified, but also taught and developed. The idea that individuals have inherent creative potential that can be developed systematically is vital to an adaptive society (Runco, 2014). Hence, a diversity of strategies and training programs have been designed that are aimed at developing creative problem solving skills, regarded as the incentive for ideas that are both effective and original (Runco & Jaeger, 2012). The notion that creativity can be taught and fostered in individuals has far-reaching implications for the changing workforce. In fact, the implication is that creativity can be supported and applied across all levels of the workforce. This alters the view that creativity is a set attribute found in a few, restricted to management or a skill that cannot be developed, but has potential for all levels of the global workforce. Creative potential has no borders and is only limited by expectations and support of the current social and cultural environment's workplace.

Economics

Higher levels of cognitive skill appear to play a major role in explaining international differences in economic growth (Hanushek & Woessmann, 2016). In countries on the technological frontier, substantial numbers of scientists, engineers, and other innovators are obviously needed. But so is a labor force that has the skills needed to survive in a technologically driven economy (Hanushek & Woessmann, 2016; Hanushek, Jamison, Jamison, Eliot & Woessmann, 2008). Advanced economies compete by producing "innovative products and services at the global technology frontier using the most advanced methods" (Porter, Ketels & Delgado, 2007). High-income countries have a high capacity for innovation—and their strategies are global in scope, which requires a workforce with the skills to "translate American business models and offerings to international marketplaces," offer "cross-border perspectives and solutions," and apply "tangible skills such as language proficiency" and "skills that are less tangible, including greater sensitivity to cultural differences, openness to new and different ideas, and the ability to adapt to change (NASEM, 2016b).

A 2014 study from Adobe Systems Incorporated found a high percentage of agreement across counties that creativity drives economic growth. The sample for this study was 5000 individuals, eighteen years and older, with 1000 participants from each country. Participants identified creativity as the key to driving economic growth. An interesting point from this study is the belief that creativity is important for future economic growth across countries. Figure 1 shows the percentage of participants from each country who indicated that creativity is important and a key to the future.

Figure 1. Percentage of participants from each country in from the Adobe Systems Incorporated 2014 study who indicated creativity is important and a key to the future

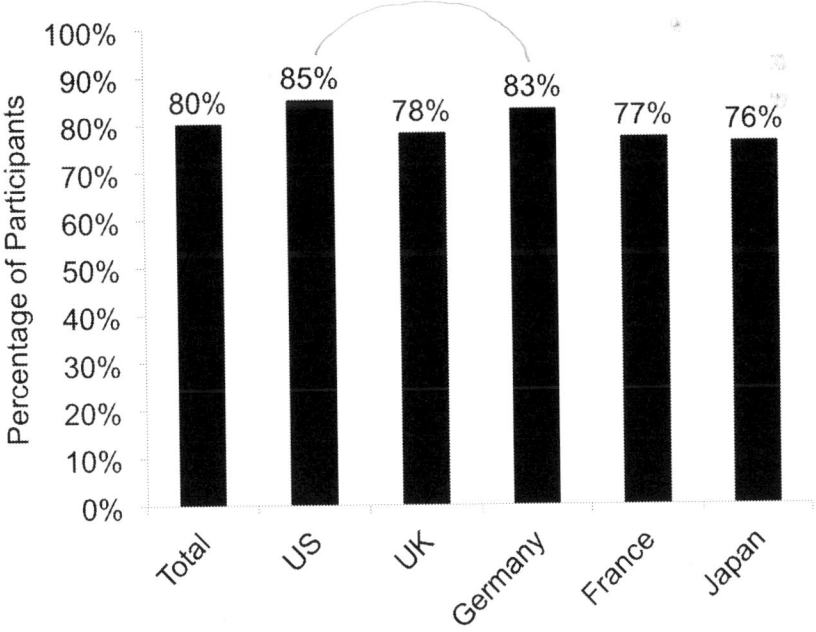

Creativity and entrepreneurial thinking is a skill set highly associated with job creation, critical thinking and problem solving skills (Pink 2005; Robinson 2006; Sternberg & Lubart, 1996). Hanushek, Jamison, Jamison, Eliot & Woessmann (2008) identify these as "cognitive skills," and believe they differentiate the economic leaders from the laggards among 50 countries from 1960 to 2000. Among other benefits, a highly skilled work force can raise economic growth by about two-thirds of a percentage point every year. Worldwide, the average annual Gross Domestic Product (GDP) growth rate for more than half a century is 2 to 3 percent, so this is a significant boost. Those countries that produce the most important new products and services can capture a premium in world markets that will enable them to pay high wages to their citizens (National Center on Education and the Economy, 2007).

Business

There is hardly a business mission statement that does not herald creativity, or a CEO who does not laud it (Breen, 2014). Employers across the United States cited professionalism/work ethic, oral and written communications, teamwork, collaboration, critical thinking, and problem solving skills as the most important skills that recently hired graduates from high school and two and four-year postsecondary institutions need, according to a nationwide survey of 400 employers (Partnership for 21st Century Skills, 2008). The acceptance of the importance of creativity in the world of business indicates that this idea maybe more than a passing phase. CEOs from around the world cited "the rapid escalation of complexity" as the biggest challenge confronting them and their organizations. These same CEOs identified creativity as "the single most important leadership competency for enterprises seeking a path through this complexity" (Dragoon, 2010). Business is actually a very creative form of art- it integrates creativity and imagination (business plans and ideas), people skills (interactions with others is imperative to business, organizational skills (organization is important in all aspects of business), and requires a focus and drive similar to that which many artists possess (Ray & Myers, 1989).

Edelman Berland's (2012) online survey of 1,068 hiring managers, *Seeking Creative Candidates: Hiring for the Future,* commissioned by Adobe (2014), underscores the importance of creativity in the workplace. The data, analyzed in 2014, indicates that both the marketplace and technology are changing the evaluation criteria for candidates and increasing the need for creativity in problem-solving. Key findings from this 2014 study are:

- Seventy-five percent of hiring managers agree the job market will change significantly in the next five years. Tech-savvy (88 percent), the ability to communicate through digital and visual media (82 percent) and creativity (76 percent) are cited as becoming essential skills.
- Hiring managers indicate that problem-solving skills and critical thinking (58 percent) and creativity and innovation (41 percent) will be among the most "in-demand" skills over the next 12 months, along with technical/specialist skills (45 percent).
- Ninety-four percent agree that creativity is key when evaluating candidates and prefer those with creative skills over conventional skills by more than 5 to 1.
- Eighty-two percent of hiring managers say they seek well-rounded candidates who are able to creatively apply core skills to a range of business and technical problems.
- Hiring managers note that students and recent graduates can set themselves apart by developing a broad range of skills (60 percent) and increasing their focus on creative thinking – learning what makes their creative wheels turn (47 percent), understanding that innovation and creativity can be learned (35 percent) and recognizing that thinking creatively will take them further than technical expertise (35 percent).
- Hiring managers agree that preparing students for the future requires a more modern approach, including courses and training opportunities to prepare students for the jobs of tomorrow (54 percent), rewarding innovation and creativity in education and on the job (38 percent) and requiring technical majors take courses in creative disciplines (33 percent; Adobe Systems Incorporated, 2014).

Healthcare

Similar to other workforce changes the health care industry is calling for creativity and innovation across the board. As early as 2003 demands for creative and innovative changes to the nursing profession were recognized. Nursing leaders must embrace innovation and engage newer strategies for responding to the changing demands for nursing practices (O'Grady, 2003). Preparing for the future of such practices calls for concerted, yet progressive action. Joel Dudley, (2014), director of biomedical informatics for Icahn School of Medicine at Mount Sinai Medical Center in New York City, claims creativity can help break down the artificial barriers that we have in medicine. In an interview, he states "We see medical specialties as being very different and very disconnected from each other—and they are largely driven by diseases. This leads to the idea that different parts of the body and different diseases are all disconnected. But we know that it's all connected. It creates these very artificial barriers that need to be broken down. Creativity with data has the potential to change the field of health as we know it (Dudley, 2014)."

The fact of the matter is- when it comes to the health of our population and the state of healthcare in this country today, we need fresh ideas. Stakeholders agree that we not only need to look for solutions by working together (e.g., payers with providers), but that we need to connect ideas from different fields and learn from experiences in other industries (Fromherz, 2012). From that perspective, unexpected companies actually have a rather large role to play in healthcare. As several speakers at the World Health Care Congress (WHCC) pointed out, the issue is not that we are lacking critical technology. Instead, we have a wealth of technologies developed in other, further advanced fields that can be applied to healthcare, if only we bring the technologies together through the creative cooperation of subject matter experts (Fromherz, 2012).

There has been support for creativity in medical training dating at least back to the eighties. Barrows and Tamblyn (1980), for example, recommended andrological approaches such as problem-based learning be used in medical schools. It was accepted in many medical schools that new approaches to medical training were needed to optimize understanding the rapid changes in medicine. According to Steven Jones (1980) learning through problem-solving is much more effective for creating in a student's mind a body of knowledge useable in the future than the traditional memory-based learning. This work supports that physician skills most important for patients are problem-solving skills, not memory skills. The principle reason we recommend devoting precious curricular time to creative endeavors is because it helps medical students become better doctors (Green, Myers, Watson, Czerwiec, Shapiro & Draus, 2016).

Not only is creativity important during medical training, but also in terms of students' future careers as doctors, continued creative development may enhance their professional practice. Students will, for example, be engaging with complexity and uncertainty, facing new problems never encountered before, making sense of patient narratives and explaining diagnoses or lack of them, hopefully in ways that are useful to patients (Thompson, Lamont-Robinson, & Younie, L., 2010). As such, creativity is not a luxury; but rather it is an essential component of the innovation on which the future of our health services depends (Thompson, Lamont-Robinson, & Younie, L., 2010).

Issues, Controversies, and Problems

Seven in ten managers agree that students are unprepared and lack the necessary skills for success both in school as well as future careers beyond schooling (Adobe Systems Incorporated, 2014). Hiring managers agree that preparing students for the future requires an innovative approach which includes: courses and training opportunities to prepare these future workers, rewarding innovation and creativity in education, on the job experience and training, and requiring technical majors take courses in creative disciplines (Adobe Systems Incorporated, 2014). These characteristics involve not only the need for adjustment but also the ability to anticipate the advent of future innovations (MacLaren, 2012; Miller & Mumford, 2014).

The evidence to support the importance of creativity from business websites is vast and far too much to adequately cover in one book. A snapshot of blogs from CEOS are discussed subsequently. Barbara Dyer, (2015) president and CEO of The Hitachi Foundation talks about the energy level change in creative work environments. In other words, when you walk into a creative workplace – you can sense it. There is a buzz in the air; the spaces are often playfully unorthodox, and people are energetic and engaged. The energy and engagement of workers in such environments leads to new ideas, creativity, and innovation. Nancy Brown, (2015) CEO of the American Heart Association claims that most people are far more creative than they give themselves credit for. In her experience, if people are given the time and opportunity to express themselves, the ideas and insights they put forward are truly eye opening. John Dragoon, (2010), senior vice president, chief marketing officer and channel chief at Novell identifies a major goal as cultivating creativity to embrace experimentation.

The United States has long recognized that the nation's prosperity and security depend on how we address challenges of disasters, poverty, famine, and disease around the world. The U.S. Agency for International Development (USAID) has played a vital role in promoting U.S. national and international interests by advancing strategies for employing science, technology, and innovation to respond to global challenges in the health industry (NASEM, 2017b). Science, technology, and innovation rely on an enabling environment that, among other things, increases incentives for including informed risk-taking and learning throughout the planning process.

SOLUTIONS AND RECOMMENDATIONS: TWENTY-FIRST CENTURY SKILLS AND A NEW VISION FOR EDUCATION

International agencies like the National Advisory Committee on Creative and Cultural Education emphasize the declining indicators of creativity in students (Robinson, 1999; 2006). Today's society demands creative and novel resolutions, and valuable ideas, adaptation and vision to bring about change (Johnston & Bate, 2013; Saracho, 2002; Runco 2006). Perhaps the strongest indicator or the sustainability of the need for creativity and innovation comes from the work of The Partnership for 21st Century Skills (2008), who emerged as the leading advocacy organization focused on infusing 21st century skills into education. This work evolved from the concern that students were not prepared for college and careers. The organization brought together the business community, education leaders and policymakers to define a powerful vision for 21st century education to ensure every child's success as citizen and worker in the 21st century. The Partnership encourages schools, districts and states to advocate for the infusion of 21st century skills into education and provides tools and resources to help facilitate and drive change.

The Framework for 21st Century Learning (P21, 2007) was developed with input from teachers, education experts, and business leaders to define and illustrate the skills and knowledge students need to succeed in work, life and citizenship, as well as the support systems necessary for 21st century learning outcomes (see Figure 2 for a diagram of the framework). It has been used by thousands of educators and hundreds of schools in the U.S. and abroad to put 21st century skills at the center of learning.

The center of the arch in the diagram above represents the demand for creativity and innovation, critical thinking and problem solving and communication and collaboration as a core value for the development of college and career ready students. Learning and innovation skills increasingly are being recognized as the skills that separate students who are prepared for increasingly complex life and work environments in the 21st century, and those who are not. A focus on creativity, critical thinking, communication and collaboration is essential to prepare students for the future (Shah, 2013). It is how well one can think for oneself and actually apply creative thinking that separates one from everyone else. When most people out there see a problem, they just complain about it instead of trying to resolve it because they never had to use their creativity to problem shoot before (Elite Daily Staff, 2013).

The Case for Creativity and Innovation

Figure 2. Framework for 21st century learning © Partnership for 21st Century Learning (P21), www.P21.org/Framework

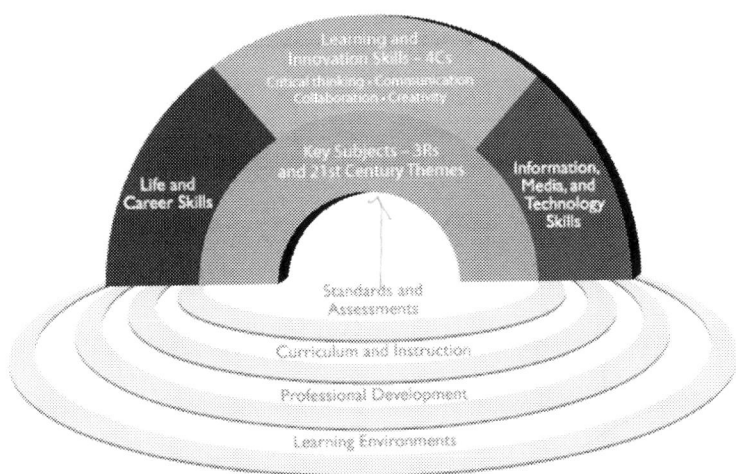

Included in the 21st Century recommendations report (Partnership for 21st Century Skills, 2008) are support documents for identifiers for creativity and innovation support. These are as follows.

Think Creatively

- Use a wide range of idea creation techniques (such as brainstorming)
- Create new and worthwhile ideas (both incremental and radical concepts)
- Elaborate, refine, analyze and evaluate their own ideas in order to improve and maximize creative efforts

Work Creatively With Others

- Develop, implement and communicate new ideas to others effectively
- Be open and responsive to new and diverse perspectives; incorporate group input and feedback into the work
- Demonstrate originality and inventiveness in work and understand the real-world limits to adopting new ideas
- Act on creative ideas to make a tangible and useful contribution to the field in which the innovation will occur

- View failure as an opportunity to learn; understand that creativity and innovation is a long-term, cyclical process of small successes and frequent mistakes
- *Implement Innovations*

Partnership for 21st Century Skills, (2008)

FUTURE RESEARCH DIRECTIONS

This chapter has emphasized that there is a desperate need for people to consistently engage in creative and critical thinking processes and that this need will not disappear anytime soon. In fact, the need will likely increase exponentially in the future. Such creative processing is not only important to everyday lives, but also in a variety of careers and disciplines that make up the current and future workforce. Because there is such a strong demand for creativity and creative thinking across different industries- there needs to be more research to support the correlation between creative outcomes and successful planned goals that lead to those outcomes. In order to better understand how creative outcomes in various domains come to be, we must better understand the goals and processes that result in those outcomes.

It is intuitive to think that creativity and novel solutions are an important part of being a global force to be reckoned with and many researchers emphasize how important creative processing is. Speculating that creativity is an important and necessary element of successful entrepreneurship and theorizing why that might be the case is useful to drive the point home, but empirical evidence to support the need for and implications of creativity and work productivity should be added to the existing research base.

CONCLUSION

Is creativity a buzzword, a trend, nothing more than a passing phase? Or, instead, is it a long-lasting and necessary element for successful endeavors? In fact, inspiring, sustaining and applying creativity is necessary to compete in today's breathlessly evolving marketplace. Tacy Trowbridge (Adobe Systems Incorporated, 2014), group manager of Adobe's education programs, claims that creativity is essential and is no longer an elective in the world of work. Further, developing a creative and focused imagination is key to creating a more ethical corporate culture as ethical choices may not be A or B and decision makers must be capable of supporting new approaches to old problems- they must create an option C (Hartmen, 2015).

According to Adobe, a leader on the forefront of innovation, creativity in the workplace starts with creativity in education (DiBenedetto, 2015). In Emily St. John Mandel's (2014) novel, *Station Eleven*, the prevailing literary motto that survival is insufficient refers to the fine arts after a flu pandemic. In this book a nomadic group of actors roam the scattered outposts of the Great Lakes region, risking everything for art and humanity. Mandel's book explores relationships that sustain us, creativity, and art at the core. We believe that survival is insufficient in the education arena if we are to move forward in the workplace. Creativity, the process, must thrive if we are to avoid a pandemic of an underprepared workforce and antiquated educational systems. If we continue to use a narrow definition of creativity we limit the potential of the workforce to move forward on the continuum of progress needed to thrive in the ever-changing world of business, medicine, education and future careers. If we accept the idea that creativity is a fixed attribute, we limit the possibility that creative thinking and innovation can and will be supported and intentionally developed.

Creativity and the innovation that spawns from creative thinking are the kinds of skills that are increasingly critical to 21st century college and career success. These are necessary components for a future workplace where the rapid force of change is evident.

REFERENCES

P21 Partnership for 21st Century Learning. (2007). *Framework for 21st century learning.* Retrieved from http://www.p21.org/our-work/p21-framework

Adobe Systems Incorporated. (2014). *Seeking Creative Candidates: Hiring for the Future New insight into hiring managers' attitudes and beliefs about the skills required for success in the workplace of tomorrow.* Retrieved from http://wwwimages.adobe.com/content/dam/Adobe/en/education/pdfs/creative-candidates-study-0914.pdf?scid=social33256266

ADP Research Institute. (2016a.). *ADP national employment report.* Retrieved from http://www.adpemploymentreport.com/2016/January/NER/NER-January-2016.aspx

ADP Research Institute. (2016b). *The evolution of work: The changing nature of the global workforce.* Retrieved from https://adobeindd.com/view/publications/5b54e57c-d9f9-44f6-aff0-fcbcadbb59c8/jvo1/publication-web-resources/pdf/ADP_Evolution_of_Work_eBook_Final.pdf

Barrows, H. S., & Tamblyn, R. M. (1980). *Problem-based learning: An approach to medical education.* New York: Springer.

Berland, E. (2012). *Creativity and education: Why it matters.* Adobe Systems Incorporated. Retrieved from http://www.adobe.com/aboutadobe/pressroom/pdfs/Adobe_Creativity_and_Education_Why_It_Matters_study.pdf

Breen, B. (2014). *The six myths of creativity.* Retrieved from https://www.fastcompany.com/51559/6-myths-creativity

Bronson, P., & Merryman, A. (2010, July 7). The Creativity Crisis. *Newsweek.* Retrieved from www.thedailybeast.com/newsweek/2010/07/10/the-creatvity-crisis.html

Brown, N. (2015). *Why you absolutely need creative employees.* Retrieved from http://fortune.com/2015/08/05/nancy-brown-creative-thinking-at-work

Cheng, C. Y., Burks, J. S., & Lee, F. (2009). Connecting the dots within creative performance and identity integration. *Psychological Science, 19*(11), 1177–1183. PMID:19076491

Chuang, S. F. (2013). Essential skills for leadership effectiveness in diverse workplace development. *Journal for Workforce Education., 6*(1), 1–23.

DiBenedetto, B. (2015). *Adobe: Unleashing creativity in the workplace.* Retrieved from http://www.triplepundit.com/special/creativity-social-innovation/adobe-unleashing-creativity-in-the-workplace/

Dragoon, J. (2010). *What is creativity's value—In marketing, in business?* Retrieved from http://www.forbes.com/2010/10/04/facebook-zuckerberg-twitter-wendy-kopp-creativity-advertising-cmo-network.html

Dudley, J. (2014). *Why health care needs creative thinking more than ever.* Retrieved from https://www.fastcoexist.com/3027327/why-health-care-needs-creative-thinking-more-than-ever

Dyer, B. (2015). *Why creativity is absolutely crucial in the workplace.* Retrieved from http://fortune.com/2015/08/23/barbara-dyer-importance-of-creativity-at-work/

Elite Daily Staff. (2013). *Why creativity is the most important quality you have*. Retrieved from http://elitedaily.com/money/entrepreneurship/creativity-important-quality/

Florida, R. (2006). *The flight of the creative class: The new goal competition for talent*. New York: Harper Collins.

Freelancers Union. (n.d.). *Freelancing in America: A National Survey of the New Workforce*. Retrieved from https://fu-web-storage-prod.s3.amazonaws.com/content/filer_public/7c/45/7c457488-0740-4bc4-ae45-0aa60daac531/freelancinginamerica_report.pdf

Fromherz, M. (2012). *Creativity leads to unexpected healthcare breakthroughs*. Retrieved from http://www.forbes.com/sites/danmunro/2012/05/14/creativity-leads-to-unexpected-healthcare-breakthroughs/#32cd6c8b7f85

Green, M.J., Myers, K., Watson, K., Czerwiec, M.K., Shapiro, D. & Draus, S. (2016). Creativity in medical education: The value of having medical students make stuff. *Journal of Medical Humanities, 37*(4), 475-483. DOI:10.1007/s10912-016-9397-1

Hanushek, E. A., Jamison, D. T., Jamison, E. A., & Woessmann, L. (2008, Spring). Education and economic growth. *Education Next, 8*(2), 62–70.

Hanushek, E.A. & Woessmann, L. (2016). Knowledge capital, growth, and the East Asian miracle. *Science, 35*(6271), 344-345.

Hartman, L. P. (2015). *4 ways to stop worrying and embrace creative risks*. Retrieved from http://fortune.com/2015/08/11/laura-pincus-hartman-creativity-in-the-workplace/

Huber, G. (2004). *The necessary nature of future firms*. Thousand Oaks, CA: Sage.

International Labor Organization. (2013). *Global employment trends 2013: Recovering from a second jobs dip*. Geneva, Switzerland: Author.

Jobs, S. (1982). *Steve Jobs speech at Golden Plate Awards*. Academy of Achievement Speech. Retrieved from https://genius.com/Steve-jobs-academy-of-achievement-speech-1982-annotated

Johnston, R. E., & Bate, J. D. (2013). *The power of strategy innovation: a new way of linking creativity and strategic planning to discover great business opportunities*. New York, NY: AMACOM.

Jones, S. (1980). Problem-based learning. An approach to medical education. New York: Springer.

King, S. (1982). *The dark tower series*. New York: Scribner.

MacLaren, I. (2012). The contradictions of policy and practice: Creativity in higher education. *London Review of Education, 10*(2), 159–172. doi:10.1080/14748460.2012.691281

Mandel, E. S. J. (2014). *Station eleven*. Toronto: Harper.

McCarthy, N. (2016). *The world's most creative cities*. State of Create: Adobe. Retrieved from https://www.statista.com/chart/6578/the-worlds-most-creative-cities/

Miller, A. L., & Mumford, A. D. (2014). Creative cognitive processes in Higher Education. *The Journal of Creative Behavior, 48*, 1–17. doi:10.1002/jocb.77

National Academies of Sciences, Engineering, and Medicine (NASEM). (2016a). *Developing a National STEM Workforce Strategy: A Workshop Summary*. Washington, DC: The National Academies Press. doi: 10.17226/21900

National Academies of Sciences, Engineering, and Medicine (NASEM). (2016b). *Promising practices for strengthening the regional STEM workforce development ecosystem*. Washington, DC: The National Academies Press.

National Academies of Sciences, Engineering, and Medicine (NASEM). (2017a). *Review of Science, Technology, Innovation, and Partnership (STIP) For Development and Implications for the Future of USAID*. Washington, DC: The National Academies Press. doi: 10.17226/24617

National Academies of Sciences, Engineering, and Medicine (NASEM). (2017b). *Advancing Concepts and Models for Measuring Innovation: Proceedings of a Workshop*. Washington, DC: The National Academies Press. doi: 10.17226/23640

National Center on Education and the Economy. (2007). *Tough choices or tough times: The report of the new commission on the skills of the American workforce*. Washington, DC: Author.

O'Grady, P. (2003). Innovation and creativity in a new age for health care. *The Journal of the New York State Nurses' Association, 34*(2), 4–8. PMID:14639775

Organization for Economic Co-operation and Development (OECD). (2013). *OECD skills outlook.* Retrieved from http://skills.oecd.org/OECD_Skills_Outlook_2013.pdf

Partnership for 21st Century Skills. (2008). *21st Century skills, education and competitiveness: A resource and policy guide.* Tucson, AZ: Author.

Pink, D. H. (2005). *A whole new mind: Why right-brainers will rule the Future.* New York: Riverhead Hardcover.

Porter, M. E., Ketels, C., & Delgado, M. (2007). *The microeconomic foundations of prosperity: Findings from the business competitiveness index.* The Global Competitiveness Report 2007–2008. The World Economic Forum.

Rabotapi, Z. L. (2012). *Why nurturing creativity is necessary for innovation.* Retrieved from http://memeburn.com/2012/07/why-nurturing-creativity-is-necessary-for-innovation/

Ray, M., & Myers, R. (1989). *Creativity in business.* New York: Doubleday.

Rietzchel, E., & Caniels, M. (2013). A special issue of creativity and innovation management: Creativity and innovation under constraints. *Creativity and Innovation Management, 22*(1), 100–102. doi:10.1111/caim.12010

Robinson, K. (1999). *All our futures: Creativity, culture and education. A report to the Department of Education and Employment, Department for Culture, Media and Sport.* London: Department of Education and Employment.

Robinson, K. (2006). *Do schools kill creativity?* Presentation at TED2006 Conference, Monterey, CA.

Runco, M. A. (2006). The development of children's creativity. In B. Spodek & N. Saracho (Eds.), *Handbook of the research on the education of young children* (pp. 121–131). Mahwah, NJ: Erlbaum.

Runco, M. A. (2014). *Creativity; Theories and themes: Research, development and practice.* San Diego, CA: Academic Press.

Runco, M. A., & Jaeger, G. J. (2012). The standard definition of creativity. *Creativity Research Journal, 24*(1), 92–96. doi:10.1080/10400419.2012.650092

Runco, M. A., Lubart, T. I., & Getz, I. (2012). Creativity and economics. In M. A. Runco (Ed.), *The creativity research handbook* (Vol. 2, pp. 173–198). New York: Hampton Press.

Saracho, O. N. (2002). Young children's creativity and pretend play. *Early Child Development and Care, 172*(5), 431–438. doi:10.1080/03004430214553

Shah, A. (2013). 21st century skills, education & competitiveness: A resource and policy guide. Washington, DC: Partnership for 21st Century Skills.

SHRM Foundation. (2015). *What's next: Future global trends affecting your organization.* Retrieved from http://futurehrtrends.eiu.com/report-2015/profile-of-the-global-workforce-present-and-future/

Stanford Center on Longevity. (2013). *The aging U.S. workforce.* Retrieved from http://longevity3.stanford.edu/wp-content/uploads/2013/09/The_Aging_U.S.-Workforce.pdf

Sternberg, R. J., & Lubart, T. I. (1996). Investing in creativity. *The American Psychologist, 51*(7), 677–688. doi:10.1037/0003-066X.51.7.677

The Economist. (2013). *Measuring adult skills: What can you do?* Retrieved from http://www.economist.com/news/international/21587823-new-study-shows-huge-international-variations-skills-what-can-you-do

Thompson, T., Lamont-Robinson, C., & Younie, L. (2010). "Compulsory creativity": Rationales, recipes and results om the placement of mandatory creative endeavor in a medical undergraduate curriculum. *Medical Education Online 2010, 15,* 5394. DOI: 10.3402/meo.v15i0.5394

Vander Ark, T. (2012). *Getting smart: How digital learning is changing the world.* San Francisco, CA: Jossey Bass.

World Bank. (2015). *Gender.* Retrieved from http://data.worldbank.org/topic/gender

Chapter 2
What Is Creativity?

ABSTRACT

The mystique of creativity has many facets. There are conflicting ideas about what creativity means and often there seems to be a lot of misunderstanding about the nature of creative people. The authors believe that creativity has many layers and can be applied across multiple domains to support the workplace and the potential of the workforce. In this chapter, the authors will discuss the definitions of creativity and connections to innovation, identify how the many facets of creativity might impact the workplace and workforce, and some common myths/misconceptions about creativity and innovation that might influence the general perceptions about creative people and their place in traditional work environments. The purpose of this chapter is to explore the perceptions about and meaning of creativity.

INTRODUCTION: THE NATURE OF CREATIVITY

A well know Indian folktale, *Six Blind Men and an Elephant*, (n.d.) tells the story of six blind men who have the opportunity to feel an elephant for the first time. Every one of them touched the elephant but a different part.

"Hey, the elephant is a pillar," said the first man who touched his leg.
"Oh, no! it is like a rope," said the second man who touched the tail.
"Oh, no! it is like a thick branch of a tree," said the third man who touched the trunk of the elephant.

"It is like a big hand fan" said the fourth man who touched the ear of the elephant.
"It is like a huge wall," said the fifth man who touched the belly of the elephant.
"It is like a solid pipe," Said the sixth man who touched the tusk of the elephant.

They began to argue about the elephant and every one of them insisted that he was right. A wise man was passing by and he saw this. He stopped and asked them, "What is the matter?" They said, "We cannot agree to what the elephant is like." Each one of them told what he thought the elephant was like. The wise man calmly explained to them, "All of you are right. The reason every one of you is telling it differently is because each one of you touched the different part of the elephant. So, actually the elephant has all those features that you all said" (Six Blind Men, n. d.)

Creativity is much like the way the men viewed the elephant in this folktale, as there are many ideas about what the nature and definition of creativity are, and each has some element of accuracy. The research about creativity has a long and seemingly conflicting history. It is probable that various researchers emphasize certain facets of creativity in their definitions because of the context of their work. In this chapter the authors will discuss the definitions of creativity and connections to innovation, identify how the many facets of creativity might impact the workplace and workforce, and some common myths/misconceptions about creativity and innovation that might influence the successful development and support for these important attributes.

Objectives

After reading this chapter one should develop an understanding of the complexity of creativity. The reader should see there are multiple definitions of creativity and gain a better understanding of how these influence the perceptions of and interactions with creative employees. In addition, the reader should gain perspectives about the misconceptions and myths surrounding creativity that may influence the development and sustainability of a productive workplace.

BACKGROUND: A GEM WITH MANY FACETS

Creativity is just connecting things. When you ask creative people how they did something, they feel a little guilty because they didn't really do it, the just saw something. It seemed obvious to them after a while. That's because they were able to connect experiences they've had and synthesize new things. And the reason they were able to do that was that they've had more experiences or they have thought more about their experiences than other people. - Steve Jobs (1995)

Trying to capture the nature of creativity in one definition is almost an antithesis to the essence of the concept. For creativity comes in many forms, is fluid, and can change with age and experience. Indeed, it is a highly complex and multidimensional in nature. (Blake, & Giannangelo, 2012). The concept of "creativity" has been widely researched for more than 50 years (Lynch & Harris, 2001). There are many reviews of creativity literature and research (e.g., Anderson, 1959a, 1959b; Glover, Ronniug, & Reynolds, 1989; Isaksen, 1987; Isaksen, Murdock, Firestein, & Treflinger, 1993; Gronhaug & Kaufmann, 1988; Runco, 2006; Saracho, 2002; Sternberg, 1988; 2006; Taylor & Getzels, 1975; Welsch, 1975). Yet there remains disagreement among researchers as to what creativity is and how it develops (Lynch & Harris, 2001).

The field of creativity, as identified through and into the 21st century, is accredited to Torrance (1962) and Guilford (1950). Guilford (1950; 1975; 1977) was one of the major influencing forces and fires behind an increased research into creativity. Torrance (1962; 1972; 1981; 1995) was considered the father of modern creativity. Along the way, it became evident as many other professionals studied creativity that is was much like a gem- a multi-faceted phenomenon rather than as a unitary construct capable of a single precise definition. As the creativity research base grew theorists accepted this idea and attempts have been made to categorize aspects of this illusive skill. The authors propose that creativity, while hard to define, can be clarified and there are elements that can be identified to support the workplace environment.

Creativity characterizes such performances as rational thinking; high levels of emotional development or feelings; talent and high levels of mental and physical development; and higher levels of consciousness, resulting in use of imagery, fantasy, and breakthroughs to the preconscious or unconscious states (Saracho, 2002). Creativity is possible in all areas of human activity, including the arts, sciences, at work, at play, and in all other areas of daily life. Tests of creativity measure not only the number of alternatives that people can generate, but also the uniqueness of those alternatives. The ability to generate multiple alternatives or to see things uniquely does not occur by chance, it is linked to other, more fundamental qualities of thinking, such as flexibility, tolerance of ambiguity or unpredictability, and the enjoyment of things heretofore unknown (Iyer, 2015). These thinking processes are vital for the future workforce as they exemplify the cognitive link to innovation.

Creativity Complexity

According to Webster, creativity is defined as the ability to produce something new through imaginative skill, whether a new solution to a problem, a new method or device, or a new artistic object or form (Creativity, 2013). The term generally refers to a richness of ideas and originality of thinking, imagination, resourcefulness, inspiration and ingenuity. Even these "simplistic" definitions are particularly complex. For example, are there criteria for the "something new" mentioned in Webster's definition? How rich do ideas have to be to count as creative? Questions such as these highlight examples of the complexities of defining creativity.

One reason a single definition of creativity is so difficult to find may be that there are so many definitions and interpretations of what the concept of creativity means. Further, definitions of creativity are often not straightforward, and many writers have contributed to the debate about what constitutes creativity, often hotly contesting different views (Sharp, 2004). One organizational scheme by Rhodes (1961) is the "4 P's" of creativity. He attempted to group creativity into four areas with support from identified theorists. These are as follows.

- **Person:** The traits, abilities, motivational and affective states, and behaviors that appear to be correlated with creativity such as the work of Barron and Harrington (1981) and Amabile (1990), Amabile & Gryskiewicz (1989).
- **Process:** The cognitive and social dynamics governing the generation, expression, and acceptance or adaptation of new ideas (e.g. Csikszenmihalyi, 2003; Martindale & Hasenfus, 1978; Runco, 1991).
- **Press:** Pressures in the social and material environment that enhance or inhibit creativity (Murray, 1938), such as access to resources, family or organizational structure, support for and valuing of originality, or the need to find solutions to urgent problems (e.g., Amabile, 1996; Amabile & Gryskiewicz, 1989; Sulloway, 1996; Witt & Beorkrem, 1989).
- **Product:** Studies of creative outputs such as publications, patents or art works (Gardner, 1999; Simonton, 1984).

What Is Creativity?

Where definitions of creativity differ most strikingly, according to Sharp (2004), is the extent to which their proponents are attempting to identify creativity as a generic human characteristic, or to define what makes highly creative people special and different from others. This is the distinction between what the report by Robinson (1999) calls the "democratic," as opposed to the "elite," definition of creativity. Howard Gardner (1999) supports the elite definition of creativity when he argues that truly creative people are those who make a difference to the world (e.g., by moving forward thinking in science, social science, music, or art). However, approaching creativity as a thinking process and a generic human characteristic changes the view of the potential and presence of creativity in the workplace. The report of the National Advisory Committee for Creative and Cultural Education, chaired by Professor Ken Robinson (Robinson, 1999) adopted a democratic view as it argued that this was the most useful way of viewing creativity in relation to education.

Despite many attempts to define creativity, a single unitary definition still eludes us. Much like the elephant in the Indian folktale, creativity can appear to be many different things depending on which part is being explored.

Cross Cutting Themes

Despite the apparent confusion and contradictions implied by many of the definitions, there does appear to be some agreement on a at least a few of the basic themes or strands. Most theorists agree that the creative process involves a number of components, most commonly identified as: (a) originality or the ability to come up with ideas and products that are new and unusual and see connections (related to Bloom's higher order thinking levels, 1956); (b) productivity or the ability to generate a variety of different ideas through divergent thinking and flexibility (Guildford, 1950; 1975; 1977; Torrance, 1962; 1972; 1981); (c) problem solving or the application of knowledge and imagination to a given situation explored (Renzulli,1982); (d) the ability to produce an outcome of value and worth (Gardner, 1983/2003); and (e) imagination, the illusive component that evades clear definition.

Welsch (1980) summarizes creativity as the process of generating unique products by transformation of existing products. These products, tangible and intangible, must be unique only to the creator, and must meet the criteria of purpose and value established by the creator. These elements have a direct connection to how creativity relates to motivation in the working environment.

Runco (2006) also wrote about the value of creativity as dependent on the current market. However, he proposes that original things must be effective to be creative which separates work creativity from fantasizing. Runco (2005) explored the concept of personal creativity, which supports the idea that creativity is relative to age, experiences, and environment. The fact that creativity is relative to the above mentioned factors further supports the idea that creativity can and should be nurtured in the workplace. Runco (2005) further describes creativity as a universal human capacity and an everyday activity that can be either nurtured or damaged by a wide range of social and environmental factors including information resources and technologies. We are born with creativity, what happens with it depends on the experiences and interactions of the individual through school, work or community interactions and societal norms.

Epstein's Generativity Theory

Epstein (1980) proposes that creativity is a natural category and any single definition would be imprecise. He claims creativity is not a good category for scientific analysis but, rather, that researchers can identify controlling variables that are indicators of creative thinking. His Generativity Theory, which is a formal, empirically based theory of the creative process, provides a convenient framework for understanding and analyzing a competencies-based approach to creative expression. Work from Epstein (1991; 1996; 1999) and Epstein, Kaminaka, Phan, and Uda (2013) provide a framework of creativity that identifies two generative mechanisms that support or inhibit creativity. One mechanism that affects creativity is the educational environment. The second generative mechanism to develop and sustain creativity requires intentional teaching of a set of competencies, particular skills and abilities that underlie successful performance.

The working definition of creativity includes: (a) Capturing - related to capture and preserving ideas that occur to you; (b) Challenging - challenge and failure helps stimulate new ideas and analysis of failure provides opportunity for growth; (c) Broadening - learning new things and intellectual curiosity; and (d) Surrounding - exposure to novel or ambiguous stimuli. Epstein's (1980) Generativity theory provides a theoretical framework for identifying variables to support creativity analysis. If one views the mechanisms that support or inhibit creativity a clearer process of identification emerges. This support system is important to develop and sustain creativity in the workplace.

The Generativity Theory suggests that specific skills and conditions must be present for creativity to occur. Generativity Theory also identifies and quantifies a possible process that underlies creative expression (Epstein, Kaminaka, Phan, & Uda, 2013). This supports the possibility of creating environments and interactions to develop and enhance creativity. It asserts that the process by which behaviors and ideas become interconnected is both orderly and predictable. This thinking about creativity provides a framework for support of creativity as the new expectations for a changing workforce evolve. The theory specifies conditions under which multiple repertoires of behavior are likely to compete and thus produce new behavior. It can be applied both to accelerate novel behavior and to direct it toward useful ends (Epstein, Kaminaka, Phan, & Uda, 2013). This is exactly what working environments of today and of the future need to support. The question is, what facets of creativity are needed to develop a workforce environment that supports and utilizes creativity for the maximum effect?

CONNECTING CREATIVITY TO THE WORKFORCE AND WORKPLACE

To summarize a defining guide for creativity one must connect the different characteristics and definitions that would build and sustain creativity and innovation. The authors believe that the following aspects are key to develop and sustain creativity in the workplace.

- We are born with creativity, what happens depends on the experiences and interactions of the individual (Runco, 2005).
- Specific skills and conditions must be present for creativity to occur (Epstein, 1999).
- Creativity is relative to age, experiences, and environment (Runco, 2005).
- Creativity is the process of generating unique products by transformation of existing products (Welsh, 1980).
- Creativity can be applied both to accelerate novel behavior and to direct it toward useful ends (Epstein, Kaminaka, Phan, & Uda, 2013).

These conditions make it possible for the advanced workplace to provide environments that support the continued development of creativity.

Innovation, Imagination, and Creativity

Which comes first, creativity or innovation? In this segment the authors will include ideas concerning the connections and relationships of creativity, imagination and innovation. Innovation is a new idea that is put into action- it may be a product or a process. Imagination is the thread that weaves the tapestry of creativity and innovation. The vision of what could be starts the process and guides the adaptations of creativity, which leads to innovation. Figure 1 depicts the relationship among creativity, innovation and imagination. The following sections further expands on the relationship among the three.

Creativity and Innovation

In order to be creative, one needs to be able to view things in new ways or from a different perspective. Among other things, one needs to be able to generate new possibilities or new alternatives. Innovation is the application of creative thinking. Creativity is the ability to take your energy and create something remarkable (Iyer, 2015). Whereas creativity is the front end of a process that ideally will result in innovation (Goleman, 2015), innovation is the end goal of creativity in the workplace and is developed through

Figure 1. Model of innovation development
(Blake & Burkett, 2017)

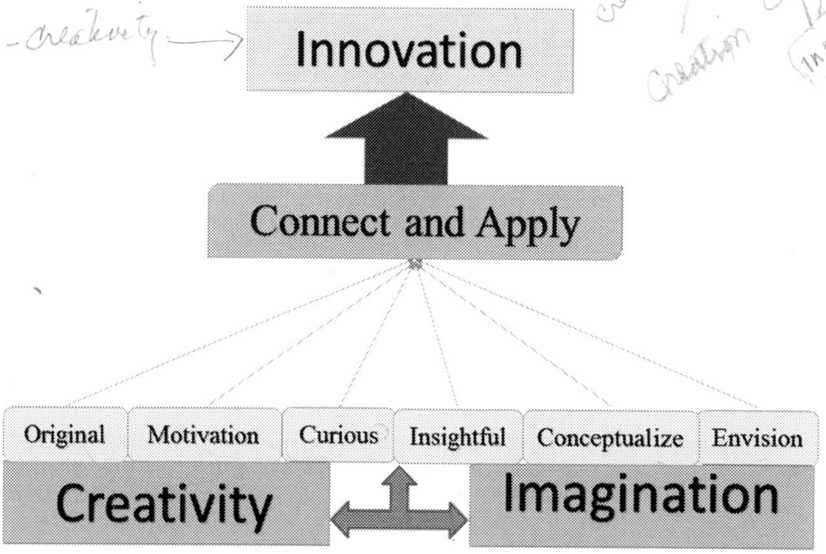

connections and applications. Everyone has creative thoughts; however, it is the application of these thoughts that produces innovated approaches to problems or the vision of the needs of the future workforce.

Creativity is a meaningful tool for generating novel and appropriate products or services to meet people's needs (Chua, Tan & Liu, 2014; Lee, Wang, Yu & Chang, 2016). Meeting people's needs is the very basis of the new vision of increasing productivity and flexibility needed in the workplace. On the other hand, innovation rarely comes from the center of the organization. It might be discussed in the boardroom, but it is rarely born there. The best ideas come to light at the edge of the organization- the area where people are connecting with people who think *differently* (Willer, 2016). This indicates that people, across all levels of the working groups, need to communicate and have discussions about ideas. A word of caution, merely talking about ideas does not necessarily identify innovation. Rather, it is the acting on and application of an idea that defines innovation.

Imagination

Imagination is perhaps the most powerful human ability, letting us create simulated realities we can explore without abandoning the real world (Brown & Vaughan, 2009). Imagination, may be called a faculty of imagining or the creative ability to form images, ideas, and sensations in the mind. Creativity, connected to imagination, characterizes such performances as rational thinking; high levels of emotional development or feelings; talent and high levels of mental and physical development; and higher levels of consciousness, resulting in use of imagery, fantasy, and breakthroughs to the preconscious or unconscious states (Saracho, 2002). Creativity refers to the utilization of imaginative thinking or ideas to produce innovation.

The interrelationship or connections of creativity and imagination set the baseline for innovation and must be encouraged, supported and rewarded in the workplace for changes to occur. In the face of rapid and constant changes with their unpredictability and inherent risks no one can continue to be complacent about the process of innovation. These conditions demand not only the need for adjustment but also the ability to anticipate the advent of future innovations (MacLaren, 2012).

Issues, Controversies, Problems: Myths and Misconceptions

In this section the authors will provide some of the common myths and misconceptions about creativity that could be influencing progress with innovation in the workplace. Perceptions of productivity or personal bias about the characteristics of creatives can influence the hiring and acceptance of ideas from workers. The operational definitions of these terms are: 1) Myth as a popular belief or tradition that has grown up around something or someone (Myth, 2013) and 2) Misconception as a false notion or a view or opinion that is incorrect because it is based on faulty thinking or understanding (Misconception, 2013). Myths and misconceptions may influence the interactions in the workplace and educational environments.

In many organizations, there is still a split between "creative" and "traditional" workers. The "creatives" are found in different departments and may look different due to expectations of the stereotypes. The US Department of Labor actually makes a distinction between traditional professions and creative professions (Weisburg, 2006). These preconceived ideas about creativity and creative people can limit the progress of education and the workplace expectations. This would limit the productivity of workers and does not connect to the new vision of the work environment. Following are some general myths or misconceptions about the nature of creativity and some more specific misconception findings about finance and the workplace. This is important as perception and expectations can often limit the potential opportunities to develop the creativity needed for innovation.

Creativity Is Genetic

The perception that creativity is innate and only found in few people has long been accepted and one of the most pervasive and stubborn myths surrounding creativity (Treffinger, Renzulli & Feldhusen, 1971). This still common perception among managers, teachers and others that some people are creative, and most are not, is just not true (See Chapter 4 in this book for a more detailed discussion). Leaders want everyone in their organization producing novel and useful ideas (Breen, 2004) and if the work environment is supportive across all levels of employees this can happen. Creative individuals are not necessarily possessed of some special characteristic called "genius" but have been given the opportunity and support to develop creative skills

(Weisberg, 1986). Almost all of the research in this field shows that anyone with normal intelligence is capable of doing some degree of creative work. Creativity depends on a number of things: experience, including knowledge and technical skills; talent; an ability to think in new ways; and the capacity to push through uncreative dry spells. Intrinsic motivation - people who are turned on by their work often work creatively - is especially critical (Breen, 2004). This stereotype was and is still very widespread in practice, especially among teachers who tend to believe that creativity is a rare trait possessed by only by an elite few students (Tabarrok, 2011).

Creative Ability Is a Fixed Attribute

Decades of research on positive training and educational effects and, lately, environmental techniques for fostering creativity strongly refute this myth (Amabile, 1983, 1996; Sternberg, 1988, 2006; Torrance, 1962, 1972, 1981, 1995; Westberg, 1996). Creative responses evolve through a straightforward series of conscious steps (Weisberg, 1993). Runco (1996) proposes that longitudinal research on trends in creativity suggests both continuities and discontinuities throughout an individual's lifespan. In other words, a child identified as highly creative in early life may or may not consistently show creativity with maturity. He argues that this uneven development may result from the fact that certain traits and talents develop at different rates and are influenced by each individual's environment and life changes. Creative expression depends on the mastery of certain competencies (or skill sets), which only a handful of people in our society - people who tend to resist socialization - ever learn (Epstein, Schmidt & Warfwel, 2008). Creativity is not a fixed attribute but can be developed or extinguished depending on environment and interactions.

Creativity Strikes Like Lightening

Creative people have flashes of insight that come from a single moment- an Aha! Or Eureka! experience. The term "Eureka" as it applies to creative discovery comes from a tale about Archimedes, a scholar from ancient Greece. He reportedly yelled "Eureka" twice after getting into a bath and noticing the water rising and "discovered" the principle of water displacement. He then realized that volume of irregular objects could be accurately measured by the amount of water displaced. They say he was so excited he jumped out of the bath and ran through the streets in Sicily sharing his flash of creative thinking. While this makes an interesting story, it is unlikely that Archimedes had this understanding from the single experience, but rather from a variety of experiences that all lead up to his Eureka! experience. According to Burkus (2014) myths like this story, and the story of Newton and his apple, connect creativity to happenstance- being in a certain place at a certain time. It is unlikely Archimedes had not been experimenting and thinking about how to measure volume of objects for a long time before the connections clicked. Epiphanies are a consequence of effort, not just the inspiration for it (Berkum, 2010).

Creative People Are Misfits

The misfit myth labels creativity as a characteristic of a person whose behavior or attitude sets them apart from others in an uncomfortably conspicuous way. This myth has been around for decade and continues to plague perceptions of creativity today. Creativity is intertwined with negative aspects of psychology and society. The "lone nut" stereotype of creativity- that of the strange, creative loner with a dark side- is surprisingly widespread (Plucker, Beghetto & Dow, 2004). Effective innovative leaders are thought to be subversives fighting the system (Zwilling, 2010) and creative people are often associated with outliers, rebels to social norms. Isaksen (1987) described this stereotype as the belief that "you must be mad, weird, neurotic or at least unusual" (p. 2) to be considered creative.

Large numbers of studies have been published on the relationship between creativity and drug use, criminality, and mental illness, with many presupposing a strong link between these deviant behaviors and conditions and creativity (e.g., Brower, 1999; Hershman & Lieb, 1998; Ludwig, 1996). Not surprisingly, these negative stereotypes reveal themselves in applied situations, hindering enhancement efforts (Plucker, Beghetto & Dow, 2004). Little of this research, however, provides conclusive evidence of strong, generalizable relationships (Plucker & Dana, 1998, 1999; Plucker & Runco, 1999).

Stories of mad geniuses who work completely alone are rarely true (Berkum, 2010), although there are some actions that may support this perception. Often, when creative ideas are first presented, they encounter resistance. The creative individual persists in the face of this resistance and eventually sells high, moving on to the next new or unpopular idea (Sternberg, 2006). Torrance (1963) described creative people as not having the time to be courteous, as refusing to take no for an answer, and as being negativistic and critical of others. According to Andreasen (2006), openness to new experiences, tolerance for ambiguity, and the way one approaches life enables creative people to perceive things in a fresh and novel way. Less creative types "quickly respond to situations based on what they have been told by people in authority," while creatives live in a more fluid and nebulous world. These characteristics place creatives outside the norm of "well behaved" individuals. Anyone different is viewed as a "misfit" in many social-cultural environments.

Creative People Are Depressive

There is some evidence to support that people with high levels of creativity experience more depression than others. Repressed creativity can express itself in unhealthy relationships, overwhelming stress, severe neurotic or even psychotic behavior, and addictive behaviors such as alcoholism (Eby, 2016). Creatives- the writers, musicians, inventors, dancers, scientists, architects, students and teachers, and any other creative type you can think of- are singled out more often than not when it comes to depression (Christensen, 2013). This is in part to how creativity develops and influences thinking. Psychologists and psychiatrists tend to agree that depression is amplified in those who tend to continually analyze their thinking. To be creative is to make sense of and connect the small details of everything one experiences, the good and the bad (Biali, 2012). Creatives naturally tend to think more, and to spend a great deal of energy thinking about their very thoughts. Andreasen (2006) claims this may partially stem from creatives' problems with filtering or gating the many stimuli that flow into the brain. For this reason, some people organize their lives in order to be isolated from human contact for long blocks of time, or at least to severely minimize human contact. Andreasen further writes that the creative person may have to confront criticism or rejection for being too questioning, or too unconventional which may lead to a feeling of isolation or not fitting in to norms. A highly original person may seem odd or strange to others, which is evident to creatives who reflect and analyze interactions continuously. Creatives know they do not fit into the norm. This is where the environment and interactions can better support the thinking that leads to innovation.

Myths From Finance and High Tech Industries

Breen in 2004 identified some issues with the structure of the finance and high tech industries' workplace There is a widespread belief, particularly in the finance and high-tech industries, that internal competition fosters innovation. The most creative teams are those that have the confidence to share and debate ideas. When people compete for recognition, they stop sharing information, which is destructive because nobody in an organization has all of the information required to put all the pieces of the puzzle together. In fact, some of the most innovate ideas come from increased collaboration. Breen (2004) provides key ideas from an interview with Teresa Amiable about her definitive research relating to creativity and innovation myths in the corporate workplace. The focus is on five different myths. These are as follows:

- Money Is a Creativity Motivator

The experimental research that has been done on creativity suggests that money isn't everything. In the study, people were asked, "To what extent were you motivated by rewards today?" Quite often they would say that the question isn't relevant- that they don't think about pay on a day-to-day basis. And the handful of people who were spending a lot of time wondering about their bonuses were doing very little creative thinking.

- Time Pressure Fuels Creativity

In one study, people often thought they were most creative when they were working under severe deadline pressure. But the 12,000 aggregate days that were studied showed just the opposite: People were the least creative when they were fighting the clock. In fact, it was found a kind of time-pressure hangover—when people were working under great pressure, their creativity went down not only on that day but the next two days as well. Time pressure stifles creativity because people cannot deeply engage with the problem. Creativity requires an incubation period; people need time to soak in a problem and let the ideas bubble up.

- Fear Forces Breakthroughs

There's this widespread notion that fear and sadness somehow spur creativity. There is even some psychological literature suggesting that the incidence of depression is higher in creative writers and artists- the depressed geniuses who are incredibly original in their thinking. But it was not supported in the population from the study. When people are excited about their work, there's a better chance that they will make a cognitive association that incubates overnight and shows up as a creative idea the next day. One day's happiness often predicts the next day's creativity.

- Competition Beats Collaboration

There's a widespread belief, particularly in the finance and high-tech industries, that internal competition fosters innovation. In Amiable's (1983, 1990, 1996) research, it was found that creativity takes a hit when people in a work group compete instead of collaborate. The most creative teams are those that have the confidence to share and debate ideas. But when people compete for recognition, they stop sharing information. And that's destructive because nobody in an organization has all of the information required to put all the pieces of the puzzle together.

- A Streamlined Organization Is a Creative Organization

Maybe it is only the public-relations departments that believe downsizing and restructuring actually foster creativity. Of course, the opposite is true: creativity suffers greatly during a downsizing. But it's even worse than realized. One study of a 6,000-person division in a global electronics company during the entire course of a 25% downsizing found every single one of the stimulants to creativity in the work environment went down significantly. Anticipation of the downsizing was even worse than the downsizing itself- people's fear of the unknown led them to basically disengage from the work. More troubling was the fact that even five months after the downsizing, creativity was still down significantly.

SOLUTIONS AND RECOMMENDATIONS

While many corporations are moving away from the old ideas about creativity, there is still much to consider concerning perceptions and beliefs about the work environment and how to support creativity. Creative process engagement is a necessary pre-condition for creative performance, and therefore encouragement of creativity and intrinsic motivation must be considered as determining factors for the extent of motivation and focus and persistence on the creative process (Amabile & Mueller, 2008; Unsworth & Clegg, 2010).

Recommendations would include developing an awareness of the myths and common misconceptions surrounding creativity, characteristics of creative people and the potential for all workers to contribute to innovation. Managers need to reflect on their beliefs about creativity and acknowledge their possible bias level concerning creatives. Moving away from old ideas of management is a must if creativity is to thrive.

FUTURE RESEARCH DIRECTIONS

There are many studies about creativity viewed from different disciplines. Researchers have a tendency to work in isolation within their specific realms, rarely crossing lines to communicate and develop research that spans domains. Future research needs to be collaborative, crossing domains to determine what levels and attributes of creativity support the development of more productive workplaces. And, conversely, what attributes of the workplace support creativity. If, after all, the goal is to generate novel, innovative thoughts, designs and products then the workplace must be designed to foster creativity.

CONCLUSION

The mystique of creativity has many facets. As the research about creativity evolved there were multiple definitions, however, almost all of the research in this field shows that anyone with normal intelligence is capable of doing some degree of creative work. Creativity depends on a number of things: experience, including knowledge and technical skills; an ability to think in new ways; and the capacity to push through uncreative dry spells. Intrinsic motivation- people who are turned on by their work often work more creatively- is especially critical (Breen, 2004). Originality is vital for creativity but not sufficient. Unusual, novel, unique and original things must be effective to be creative (Runco, 2006).

It is up to educators, CEOs, managers and other leaders to provide the environment and opportunity to develop and support creativity in the workplace. Clearly the concept of creativity is interpreted in different ways. However, in order for innovation to proceed there must be connections and actions, not just ideas. This requires opportunity for dialog across all levels of the workforce, not just from the top of the ladder.

Most everyone agrees that the goal of innovation is positive change, to make someone or something better. Entrepreneurs need it to start, and established companies need it to survive. The front end of innovation, or "ideating" is the energizing and glamorous part. Execution seems like behind-the-scenes dirty work. But without the reality of execution, big ideas go nowhere (Zwilling, 2010). There is a need for a new generation of workers who are creative and innovative. And all levels of workers across multiple domains hold the key to successful innovation.

REFERENCES

Amabile, T. M. (1983). *The Social Psychology of Creativity*. New York: Springer Verlag. doi:10.1007/978-1-4612-5533-8

Amabile, T. M. (1990). Within you, without you: The social psychology of creativity and beyond. In M. A. Runco & R. S. Albert (Eds.), *Theories of Creativity* (pp. 61–91). Newbury Park, CA: Sage Publications.

Amabile, T. M. (1996). *Creativity in Context: Update to the Social Psychology of Creativity*. Boulder, CO: Westview Press.

Amabile, T. M., & Gryskiewicz, N. D. (1989). The Creative Environment Work Scales. *Creativity Research Journal*, 2.

Amabile, T. M., & Mueller, J. S. (2008). Studying creativity, its processes, and its antecedents: An exploration of the componential theory of creativity. In J. Zhou & C. E. Shalley (Eds.), *Handbook of Organizational Creativity* (pp. 237–261). New York, NY: Erlbaum.

Anderson, H. H. (Ed.). (1959a). *Creativity and its cultivation*. Addresses presented at the interdisciplinary symposia on creating at Michigan State University. Harper & Row.

Anderson, H. H. (Ed.). (1959b). *Creativity in perspective*. In Creativity and its cultivation: Addresses presented at the interdisciplinary symposia on creativity at Michigan State University. Harper & Row.

Andreasen, N. C. (2006). *The creative brain: The science of genius*. Penguin Random House.

Barron, F., & Harrington, D. (1981). Creativity Intelligence and Personality. *Annual Review of Psychology, 32*.

Berkum, S. (2010). *The myths of innovation.* Sebastopol, CA: O'Reilly Media, Inc.

Biali, S. (2012). A little weird? Prone to depression? Blame your creative brain. *Prescriptions for Life.* Retrieved from https://www.psychologytoday.com/blog/prescriptions-life/201204/little-weird-prone-depression-blame-your-creative-brain

Blake, S., & Giannangelo, D. (2012). Creativity and Young Children: Review of Literature and Connections to Thinking Processes. In O. Saracho & B. Spodek (Eds.), *Contemporary perspectives on research in creativity in early childhood education* (pp. 289–312). Charlotte, NC: Information Age Publishing.

Bloom, B. S. (1956). Taxonomy of educational objectives.: Vol. 1. *Cognitive domain.* New York: McKay.

Breen, B. (2004). *The 6 myths of creativity.* An interview with Teresa Amabile. *Fast Company, 89*(December), 75.

Brower, R. (1999). Dangerous minds: Eminently creative people who spent time in jail. *Creativity Research Journal, 12*(1), 3–13. doi:10.1207/s15326934crj1201_2

Brown, S., & Vaughan, C. (2009). *Play: How it shapes the brain, opens the imagination, and invigorates the soul.* Penguin.

Burkus, D. (2014). *The myths of creativity: The truth about how Innovative companies and people generate great ideas.* San Francisco, CA: Jossey-Bass.

Christensen, T. (2013). *The link between depression and creativity, and how it can be good for you.* Retrieved from http://creativesomething.net/post/55508909341/the-link-between-depression-and-creativity-and

Chua, B. L., Tan, O. S., & Liu, W. C. (2014). Journey into the problem-solving process: Cognitive functions in a PBL environment. *Innovations in Education and Teaching International.* doi:10.1080/14703297.2014.961502

Creativity. (2013). In *Merriam-Webster.com.* Retrieved from http://www.merriamwebster.com/http

Csikszenmihalyi, M. (2003). The domain of creativity. In Creativity Research Handbook (vol. 3). Cresskill NJ: Hampton Press.

Eby, D. (2016). *Creativity and depression.* Retrieved from https://psychcentral.com/lib/creativity-and-depression/

Epstein, R. (1980). In Response: Defining Creativity. *The Behavior Analyst*, *3*(2), 65. doi:10.1007/BF03391845 PMID:22478482

Epstein, R. (1991). Skinner, Creativity, and the Problem of Spontaneous Behavior. *Psychological Science*, 6(6), 362–370. doi:10.1111/j.1467-9280.1991.tb00168.x

Epstein, R. (1996). *Cognition, Creativity, and Behavior: Selected Essays.* Westport, CT: Praeger.

Epstein, R. (1999). Generativity Theory. In M. A. Runco & S. Pritzker (Eds.), Encyclopedia of Creativity (pp. 759–766). Academic Press.

Epstein, R., Kaminaka, K., Phan, V., & Uda, R. (2013). How Is Creativity Best Managed? Some Empirical and Theoretical Guidelines. *Creativity and Innovation Management*, 22(4), 359–374. doi:10.1111/caim.12042

Epstein, R., Schmidt, S. M., & Warfel, R. (2008). Measuring and Training Creativity Competencies: Validation of a New Test. *Creativity Research Journal*, 20(1), 7–12. doi:10.1080/10400410701839876

Gardner, H. (1983/2003). *Frames of mind. The theory of multiple intelligences.* New York: Basic Books.

Gardner, H. (1999). *Intelligence reframed: Multiple intelligences for the 21st century.* New York, NY: Basic Books.

Glover, J. A., Ronning, R. R., & Reynolds, C. R. (Eds.). (1989). *Handbook of creativity.* New York, NY: Plenum Press. doi:10.1007/978-1-4757-5356-1

Goleman, D. (2015). *Creativity and innovation: What's the difference?* Retrieved from http://www.danielgoleman.info/daniel-goleman-creativity-and-innovation-whats-the-difference

Gronhaug, K., & Kaufmann, G. (Eds.). (1988). *Innovation: A cross-disciplinary perspective.* Oslo, Norway: Norwegian University Press.

Guilford, J. P. (1950). Creativity. *The American Psychologist*, 5(9), 444–454. doi:10.1037/h0063487 PMID:14771441

Guilford, J. P. (1975). Varieties of creative giftedness, their measurement and development. *Gifted Child Quarterly, 19*(2), 107–121. doi:10.1177/001698627501900216

Guilford, J. P. (1977). *Way beyond the IQ*. Buffalo, NY: Creative Education Foundation.

Hershman, D. J., & Lieb, J. (1998). *Manic depression and creativity*. Amherst, NY: Prometheus Books.

Isaksen, S. G. (Ed.). (1987). *Frontiers of creativity research: Beyond the basics*. Buffalo, NY: Bearly Limited.

Isaksen, S. G., Murdock, M.C., Firestein, R. L., & Tieffinger, D. I. (Eds.). (1993). Understanding and recognizing creativity: The emergence of a discipline. Norwood, NJ: Ablex.

Iyer, S. (2015). *Steve Jobs-Creativity, imagination & innovation*. Retrieved from https://www.linkedin.com/pulse/steve-jobs-creativity-imagination-innovation-sachin-iyer

Jobs, S. (1995). *Steve Jobs interview from Triumph of the nerds*. PBS. Retrieved from http://www.pbs.org/nerds/

Lee, J. C., Wang, C. L., Yu, L. C., & Chang, S. H. (2016). The effects of perceived support for creativity on individual creativity of design-majored students: A multiple-mediation model of savoring. *Journal of Baltic Science Education, 15*(2), 232–245.

Ludwig, A. M. (1996). *The price of greatness: Resolving the creativity and madness controversy*. New York: Guilford.

Lynch, M. D., & Harris, C. R. (2001). *Fostering creativity in children, K-8*. Needham Heights, MA: Allyn & Bacon.

MacLaren, I. (2012). The contradictions of policy and practice: Creativity in higher education. *London Review of Education, 10*(2), 159–172. doi:10.1080/14748460.2012.691281

Martindale, C., & Hasenfus, N. (1978). EEG differences as a function of creativity, stage of the creative process, and effort to be original. *Biological Psychology*, 6. PMID:667239

Misconception. (2013). In *Merriam-Webster.com*. Retrieved from http://www.merriamwebster.com/http

Murray, H. (1938). *Explorations in Personality*. New York, NY: Oxford University Press.

Myth. (2013). In *Merriam-Webster.com*. Retrieved from http://www.merriamwebster.com/http

Plucker, J. A., Beghetto, R. A., & Dow, G. T. (2004). Why isnt creativity more important to educational psychologists? Potentials, pitfalls and future directions in creativity research. *Educational Psychologist, 39*(2), 83–96. doi:10.1207/s15326985ep3902_1

Plucker, J. A., & Dana, R. Q. (1998). Alcohol, tobacco, and marijuana use: Relationships to undergraduate students 'creative achievement. *Journal of College Student Development, 39*, 472–481.

Plucker, J. A., & Dana, R. Q. (1999). Drugs and creativity. In M. A. Runco & S. Pritzker (Eds.), *Encyclopedia of creativity* (Vol. 1, pp. 607–611). San Diego, CA: Academic.

Plucker, J. A., & Runco, M. (1999). Creativity and deviance. In M. A. Runco & S. Pritzker (Eds.), *Encyclopedia of creativity* (Vol. 1, pp. 541–545). San Diego, CA: Academic.

Renzulli, J. S. (1982). What makes a problem real: Stalking the illusive meaning of qualitative differences in gifted education. *Gifted Child Quarterly, 26*(4), 147–156. doi:10.1177/001698628202600401

Rhodes, M. (1961). An analysis of creativity. *Phi Delta Kappan, 42*, 305–310.

Robinson, K. (1999). *All our futures: Creativity, culture and education. A report to the Department of Education and Employment, Department of Culture, Media and Sport*. London: Department of Education and Employment.

Runco, M. A. (1991). *Divergent Thinking*. Norwood, NJ: Ablex.

Runco, M. A. (1996). Personal creativity: Definition and developmental issues. *New Directions for Child and Adolescent Development, 72*(72), 3–30. doi:10.1002/cd.23219967203

Runco, M. A. (2005). Creative giftedness. In R. J. Sternberg & J. E. Davidson (Eds.), *Conceptions of giftedness* (Rev. Ed.; pp. 295–311). New York, NY: Cambridge University. doi:10.1017/CBO9780511610455.017

Runco, M. A. (2006). The development of children's creativity. In B. Spodek & N. Saracho (Eds.), Handbook of the research on the education of young children (pp. 121-131). Mahwah, NJ: Erlbaum.

Saracho, O. N. (2002). Young childrens creativity and pretend play. *Early Child Development and Care, 175*(5), 431–438. doi:10.1080/03004430214553

Sharp, C. (2004). Developing young children's creativity: What can we learn from research? *Topic, 32,* 5–12.

Simonton, D. K. (1984). *Genius, creativity and leadership: Historiometric inquiries.* Cambridge, MA: Harvard University Press. doi:10.4159/harvard.9780674424753

Six Blind Men and the Elephant. An Indian Folktale. (n.d.). Retrieved form http://www.jainworld.com/literature/story25.htm

Sternberg, R. J. (Ed.). (1988). *The nature of creativity: Contemporary psychological perspectives.* Cambridge, MA: Cambridge University Press.

Sternberg, R. J. (2006). The nature of creativity. *Creativity Research Journal, 18*(1), 87–98. doi:10.1207/s15326934crj1801_10

Sulloway, F. (1996). *Born to rebel.* New York: Pantheon.

Tabarrok, A. (2011). *Teachers don't like creative students.* Retrieved from http://marginalrevolution.com/marginalrevolution/2011/12/teachers-dont-like-creative-students.html

Taylor, I. A., & Getzels, J. W. (Eds.). (1975). *Perspectives in creativity.* New Brunswick, NJ: Transaction.

Torrance, E. (1963). *Education and the creative potential.* University of Minnesota Press.

Torrance, E. P. (1962). *Guiding creative talent.* Englewood Cliffs, NJ: Prentice Hall. doi:10.1037/13134-000

Torrance, E. P. (1972). Can we teach children to think creatively? *The Journal of Creative Behavior, 6,* 236–262. doi:10.1002/j.2162-6057.1972.tb00936.x

Torrance, E. P. (1981). Creative teaching makes a difference. In J. C. Gowan, J. Khatena, & E. P. Torrance (Eds.), *Creativity: Its educational implications* (2nd ed.; pp. 99–108). Dubuque, IA: Kendall/Hunt.

Torrance, E. P. (1995). *Why fly?* Norwood, NJ: Ablex Publishing Corporation.

Treffinger, D. J., Renzulli, J. S., & Feldhusen, J. F. (1971). Problems in the assessment of creative thinking. *The Journal of Creative Behavior, 5*(2), 104–112. doi:10.1002/j.2162-6057.1971.tb00880.x

Unsworth, K. L., & Clegg, C. W. (2010). Why do employees undertake creative action? *Journal of Occupational and Organizational Psychology, 83*(1), 77–99. doi:10.1348/096317908X398377

Weisberg, R. (1986). *Creativity: Genius and other myths.* New York, NY: WH Freeman/Times Books/Henry Holt.

Weisberg, R. (1993). *Creativity: Beyond the myth of genius.* New York, NY: Freeman.

Weisberg, R. W. (2006). *Creativity: Understanding innovation in problem solving, science, invention, and the arts.* Hoboken, NJ: John Wiley & Sons.

Welsch, G. S. (1975). *Creativity and intelligence: A personality approach.* Chapel Hill, NC: University of North Carolina at Chapel Hill, Institute for Research in Social Science.

Welsch, P. K. (1980). *The nurturance of creative behavior in educational environments: A comprehensive curriculum approach* (Unpublished doctoral dissertation). University of Michigan.

Westberg, K. (1996). The effects of teaching students how to invent. *The Journal of Creative Behavior, 30*(4), 249–267. doi:10.1002/j.2162-6057.1996.tb00772.x

Willer, P. (2016). *How to connect people to drive innovation.* Innovation Excellence. Retrieved from http://innovationexcellence.com/blog/2016/10/16/how-to-connect-people-to-drive-innovation/

Witt, L. A., & Beorkrem, M. N. (1989). Climate for creative productivity as a predictor of research usefulness and organizational effectiveness in an R&D organization. *Creativity Research Journal, 2*(1-2), 30–40. doi:10.1080/10400418909534298

Zwilling, M. (2010). Beware of these 10 myths about innovation. *Startup Professionals Musings.* Retrieved from http://www.businessinsider.com/startups-beware-of-these-10-myths-about-innovation-2010-9

Chapter 3
What Stops Creativity?

ABSTRACT

As demand for creativity increases globally the role of education is crucial to prepare future workers to deal with changing expectations of the workforce. Educational institutions should reflect intentional support for development of creativity and innovation. There is a conflicting paradigm of demands for success in the global community and the measures of academic achievement in many schools. Educational systems influence creativity and innovation through environments, socialization, and reward systems. Some specific points of interest about creativity and innovation include research on teachers' interactions and beliefs about creative students, the possible impact of a high stakes accountability system and admission requirements for teacher training.

INTRODUCTION: THE ANIMAL SCHOOL

Once upon a time the animals decided they must do something heroic to meet the problems of a "new world" so they organized a school. They had adopted an activity curriculum consisting of running, climbing, swimming and flying. To make it easier to administer the curriculum, all the animals took all the subjects. The duck was excellent in swimming. In fact, better than his instructor. But he made only passing grades in flying and was very poor in running. Since he was slow in running, he had to stay after school and also drop swimming in order to practice running. This was kept up until his webbed feet were badly worn and he was only average in swimming. But average was acceptable in school so nobody worried about that, except the

DOI: 10.4018/978-1-5225-4952-9.ch003

duck. The rabbit started at the top of the class in running but had a nervous breakdown because of so much makeup work in swimming. The squirrel was excellent in climbing until he developed frustration in the flying class where his teacher made him start from the ground up instead of the treetop down. He also developed a "charlie horse" from overexertion and then got a C in climbing and D in running. The eagle was a problem child and was disciplined severely. In the climbing class, he beat all the others to the top of the tree but insisted on using his own way to get there. At the end of the year, an abnormal eel that could swim exceeding well and also run, climb and fly a little had the highest average and was valedictorian. The prairie dogs stayed out of school and fought the tax levy because the administration would not add digging and burrowing to the curriculum. They apprenticed their children to a badger and later joined the groundhogs and gophers to start a successful private school (Reavis,1940).

This story was written when George Reavis was the Assistant Superintendent of the Cincinnati Public Schools. He was concerned with the decisions made in schools, which while well intended, often tried to mold students to fit expectations of the average or norm. His story illustrates the effect of curriculum and schools which often presume that students should become what educational systems consider a good fit for social or educational norms.

Socialization

It all starts with our education systems, which influence how the future workplace is set up as well as how companies are run and what value is placed on creativity. The first place outside the home environment where children go to share their creative thinking is school and this is where the stage is set for the future expectations of work. What happens there determines the future of economic systems through the socialization of students, which identify acceptable thinking and interactions between groups of people. Few would argue that schools are the place children go to learn, not just academics, but the sociocultural values of the governing political and economic systems.

In this chapter the authors will provide information about how schools influence creativity and innovation through environments, socialization, and reward systems. Some specific points of interest about creativity and innovation include research on teachers' interactions and beliefs about creative students, the possible impact of a high stakes accountability system and admission requirements for teacher training. The authors believe that educational environments, in the current accountability era, diminish and stop the development of creative thinking through interactions, reward systems, and biased belief systems. Recommendations to improve these issues will be included. If creativity and innovation are truly valued, there should be evidence that schools and teachers support these attributes.

Objectives

The purpose of this chapter is to inform and develop awareness of the influence of schools and educational environments on creativity. After reading this chapter the reader should be able to relate educational environments to personal creativity development and better understand how schools impact the development of creative thinking.

BACKGROUND: THE NATURE OF SCHOOLS

[In school] I encountered authority of a different kind than I had ever encountered before, and I did not like it. And they really almost got me. They came close to really beating any curiosity out of me. - Steve Jobs (n.d.)

There are many notable creative people who challenge the role of schools and creativity development. George Bernard Shaw compared school to prison, but then suggested prison might be better. He said, "There is, on the whole, nothing on earth intended for innocent people so horrible as a school. To begin with, it is a prison. But in some respects, more cruel than a prison. In a prison, for instance, you are not forced to read books written by the warders and the governor…In the prison you are not forced to sit listening to turnkeys discoursing without charm or interest on subjects that they don't understand and don't care about, and therefore incapable of making you understand or care about. In a prison, they may torture your body; but they do not torture your brains" (Shaw, n.d.).

Elmore (2012) writes that historically some of the world's most creative geniuses hated the instruction they received in school. Thomas Edison was sent home with a letter from school proclaiming he was mentally deficient and expelled from school. Rather than tell her son what the teachers had written she told him the letter stated he was a genius and the school didn't have good enough teachers to train him. He was home schooled from that point on and did became a renown genius of his time.

Einstein remembered most of his schooling in both Germany and Switzerland as an "unhappy experience." He later wrote, "It is nothing short of a miracle that the modern methods of instruction have not yet entirely strangled the holy curiosity of inquiry...without this, it goes to wreck and ruin without fail." (Einstein, n.d.)

From Thomas Edison, expelled from school for being "mentally deficient", to Einstein, to Steve Jobs, creative students do not seem to fit the mold of most schools. This may be due to the design and pedagogical approach used in schools. During the Industrial Revolution schools became a place to train workers for jobs in the "new era" of economic progress. This model supported that time in history and not current social, economic or global expectations. And this model still exists in our schools, one that trains and ingrains a socialization of passive obedience, compliance and acceptance of repetitive tasks as not just the norm, but a desired end. It basically supposes a social normalization process to make life in urban ghettos bearable, in combination with the installation of a series of abilities—tricks, if you will—during adolescence, which, once learned, are repeated over and again during the following decades until the worker either retires or, worse, becomes obsolete (Prins, 2015).

Power Shifts

The power of learning no longer relies on the teacher as the keeper of all knowledge- in fact this antiquated idea hinders support and development of creative thinking. The assessment that accompanies this approach is equally outdated and geared to lower level thinking, ignoring the cognitive demands of the 21st century. The Industrial Revolution is long over; the knowledge economy yet continues to be ignored in educational institutions. The essential value of this era is entrepreneurialism, which requires people to use their brains in entirely different ways. In order for companies and countries to stay competitive, the ways in which children and adults are being taught to think needs to be carefully examined (Giang, 2013).

Technology has had a major impact on the shifting power in educational environments as it has on the changing workforce and jobs. Teachers present their lessons while students google the information to see if the teacher is accurate. Professors post future lecture topics for classes, students google topics and then skip classes. Students can seek information about topics they consider of interest or important as opposed to the past when teachers decided what was important or should be learned. This power shift, when combined with the traditional nature and personal epistemological beliefs of teachers may create a conflict of efficiency and outcomes.

The Influence of Schools

The time spent in formal schooling varies by country and region of the world. In the United States the average is twelve years, followed by Sweden, Canada, New Zealand and Norway with more than eleven years, the top nine countries (more than ten years in schools) average 11.1 years and the next 13 countries (more than 9 years in schools) average 9.4 years (Nation Master, n.d.). While different countries require different hours per day and schools usually differentially reflect the political and cultural norms of a country, one thing is evident- that children all over the world are spending a lot in time in schools. Since learning and innovation skills increasingly are being recognized as the skills that separate students who are prepared for complex life and work environments in the 21st century, and those who are not, a focus on creativity, critical thinking, communication and collaboration is essential to prepare students for the future (Shah, 2013). Consequently, the educational institutions, schools, should reflect intentional support for development of creativity and innovation. However there seems to be a conflict between the goals of 21st education and schooling and the concern about creativity and schools has now become universal (Adobe Systems Incorporated, 2013).

CREATIVITY AND EDUCATIONAL ENVIRONMENTS

It is no secret that students in the United States are slipping in core areas such as math and science, especially when compared to other countries, such as Singapore and Finland. But what may be even more alarming is that students are losing more than just a top spot in international rankings: according to research, their capacity for creativity has been in steady decline (Bronson & Merryman, 2010; Kim, 2011; Meador,1992; Prins, 2015; Robinson,1999; Runco, 2004). The delivery systems of learning, pedagogical approaches, still reflect the need for passive compliance. Our schools fail to engage creative students because they continue to use pedagogy that was created for life fifty to one hundred years ago- lecture, drill, test (Elmore, 2012). The use of such "direct instruction," so clearly evident in many schools, ignore the innovations of the new era of learning.

One of the myths of creativity is that very few people are really creative," said Sir Ken Robinson, Ph.D., an internationally recognized leader in the development of education, creativity and innovation. The truth is that everyone has great capacities but not everyone develops them. One of the problems is that too often our educational systems do not enable students to develop their natural creative powers. Instead, they promote uniformity and standardization. The result is that we're draining people of their creative possibilities and producing a workforce that's conditioned to prioritize conformity over creativity (Robinson, 2007).

Is this a concern? For some of the more creative kids, their creativity will help them survive their standardized school years. For others, this standardization crushes their passions, spirits, and joy (Adobe Systems Incorporated, 2013). While at one time it may have been acceptable to assume the creative wheat would be separated from the chaff through education experiences, the time has passed when economic systems can take the chance of losing creative thinkers through early socialization experiences.

The creativity issue is evident across countries. In the 2012 Adobe Systems Incorporated State of Create Study (2013) an online survey was sent to 5,000 adults, 18 years or older, 1,000 each in the United States, United Kingdom, Germany, France and Japan. Many participants feel that creativity is part of their culture. It was also found that more than half of the participants feel that creativity is being stifled by their education systems. And that it is perceived that countries take creativity for granted (52% globally, 70% in the United States).

According to Randi Weingarten, the President of the American Federation of Teachers, parents overwhelmingly believe that public schools are the single most important institution for the future of their communities, their nation (2013). Yet studies indicate limited support for creativity. Meador (1992) found evidence from the United States that creativity (as measured by divergent thinking tests) declines when children enter kindergarten, at around the age of 5 or 6. Sir Ken Robinson (1999), chair of the United Kingdom government's report on creativity, education, and the economy described research that showed that young people lost their ability to think in divergent or nonlinear ways, a key component of creativity. Of 1,600 children aged three to five who were tested, 98% showed they could think in divergent ways. By the time they were aged 8 to 10, 32% could think divergently. When the same test was applied to 13- to 15- year-olds, only 10% could think in this way. In addition, when the test was used with 200,000 25-year-olds, only 2% could think divergently. Education is driven by the idea of one answer and this idea of divergent thinking becomes stifled. He described creativity as the 'genetic code' of education and said it was essential for the new economic circumstances of the 21st century. The implication of these findings is truly frightening- the longer students stay in schools the less creative they become.

The Culture of Doublethink

All education policymakers want future students to be globally competitive, to out-innovate others, and to become job-creating entrepreneurs (Zhou, Shen, Wang, Neber, & Johnii, 2013), yet academic success indicators are based on conformity and parrot-like responses to questions on standardized tests with questionable validity. This cognitive dissonance, the difference between claims of support for creative and critical thinking and the indicators of academic success has been identified as doublethink. Doublethink is "to hold simultaneously two opinions which canceled out, knowing them to be contradictory and believing in both of them," according to George Orwell, who coined the phrase in his novel *1984* (Zhoa, 2012).

Orwell (*1984*) wrote:

The power of holding two contradictory beliefs in one's mind simultaneously, and accepting both... To tell deliberate lies while genuinely believing in them, to forget any fact that has become inconvenient, and then, when it becomes necessary again, to draw it back from oblivion for just as long as it is needed, to deny the existence of objective reality and all the while to take account of the reality which one denies — all this is indispensably necessary. Even in using the word doublethink it is necessary to exercise doublethink. For by using the word one admits that one is tampering with reality; by a fresh act of doublethink one erases this knowledge; and so on indefinitely, with the lie always one leap ahead of the truth. (Orwell, 1949, p. 220)

While the authors prefer to believe that schools do not tell deliberate or intentional lies there is evidence of a discrepancy between what they say about creativity and what they do in schools. This does create a denial of objective reality where the support of creativity is concerned. To better understand doublethink and how it applies to educational environments the authors start with examples of classroom interactions and expectations. What they say is often in conflict with what they do which is where the doublethink of educational environments influences the development of creative thinking.

Doublethink: Classroom Interactions

Cropley (2001) explored educators' beliefs about creativity in the classroom. He found that when asked about the importance of fostering creativity in the classroom, 96% of teachers said it was essential. However, when practice was examined, it was found that the majority of teachers, from Grade 2 through college, tended to react negatively to the students who behaved in ways associated with a creative cognitive process. To deliver the curriculum efficiently, many teachers prefer passive student behavior and prepackaged course materials. Experimental educational environments were considered chaotic and out of control. This is evident when one observes teacher and administrators' interactions in classrooms where students are to sit and listen, not talk. Educators assess what they value and creative exploratory learning environments do not seem to be on the list of valued behavior (Blake & Giannangelo, 2012).

This idea is supported by Epstein (1991, 1996, 1999) who found that when children enter first grade, they are severely discouraged from expressing new or unusual ideas, and daydreaming is forbidden. Epstein believes that children enter formal schooling with potential creativity whereas few children express creativity by the end of first grade. Epstein further ascertains that the few people who have a tendency to resist socialization maintain their creativity in spite of the influence of educational systems. Because creative expression tends to be discouraged in our culture such expression is relatively rare (Epstein, Kaminaka, Phan, & Uda, 2013). This is true, in part, because creative expression depends on the mastery of certain competencies (or skill sets), which only a handful of people in our society—people who tend to resist socialization—ever learn. (Epstein, Schmidt & Warfwel, 2008). Our school systems make creativity the nearly exclusive property of antisocial personality types (Epstein, 1999).

In Runco's (2006) chapter in the *Handbook of Education on the Education of Young Children* he ascertains that environment plays a major role in sustaining or extinguishing creativity. By the fourth grade, children have experienced several years of formal education and have been expected to raise their hands before speaking, sit in rows, and follow a precise daily schedule.

The focus on behavior over thinking may play a role in the declining creativity development in schools.

The following chart (Table 1) gives some examples of the conflict of what they say, yet what they do, which indicates the duality and inconsistency between action and words.

It is estimated that at least two thirds of our young people don't get what they need and deserve from our schools in part because of a narrow pedagogical approach (Wai, 2012). Empirical experience indicates that the adoption of creative thinking models is possible at almost any age, especially when paying additional attention to pedagogic methods and tools that allow demolishing the walls erected by creativity inhibitors (Prins, 2015). This issue is further compounded by belief systems found in teachers about what an ideal student is.

Table 1. Examples of doublethink and creativity in education

What They Say	What They Do
Today's society demands creative and novel resolutions, and valuable ideas, adaptation and vision to bring about change. (Saracho, 2002; Runco 2006; Bronson & Merryman, 2010).	Admit teacher candidates using measures predictive of academic success and prior achievement.
Creativity involves divergent and convergent thinking, innovation, problem finding and problem solving, self-expression, intrinsic motivation, a questioning attitude, and self-confidence.	1/3 of teachers spend more than 60 percent of the school day having their students prepare for the state test (Berliner, 2009).
Cropley (2001)- Teachers say creativity is essential	From grade 2-College teachers react negatively to students who behave in ways associated with creative cognitive processes.
Andreasen (2006) Teachers say innovation and problem solving is important.	Techers reward less creative types who "quickly respond to situations based on what they have been told by people in authority."
Epstein (1991, 1996, 1999) -Teachers support the need for creativity.	School systems make creativity the nearly exclusive property of antisocial personality types. When children enter 1st grade they are discouraged from creative behavior.
Runco (2006) – Teachers know environment plays major role in sustaining or extinguishing creativity.	Teachers focus on behavior over thinking.
Teachers identify the need for creativity and innovation in students.	Kagetama (2016) - teachers prefer students who are "pleasers," over creative types.
Teachers say they want creative students.	Westby & Dawson 2010 Judgments for the favorite student were negatively correlated with creativity; judgments for the least favorite student were positively correlated with creativity.

Doublethink: Teachers' Beliefs About Creative Children

Numerous studies have found that teachers prefer students who are "pleasers," who have traits that are somewhat the opposite of creative types (Kagetama, 2016). For decades studies have indicated that teachers prefer traits that seem to run counter to creativity, such as conformity and unquestioning acceptance of authority (Bachtold, 1974; Cropley, 1992; Dettmer, 1981; Getzels & Jackson, 1962; Torrance, 1963). More recent studies indicate that teachers overwhelmingly discriminate against creative students, favoring their satisfier classmates who more readily follow directions and do what they are told (Olien, 2013). This is a concern as students' beliefs about their self-value and behavioral expectations are defined by teachers. One must realize that children can spend eleven plus years in this environment, neglected or actually punished for their creative thinking while children who conform to "good" behavior are rewarded and praised (Myers & Torrance, 1961; Stone, 1980).

Westby & Dawson (1995) describe the results of studies related to teachers' perceptions of creative students. One study was based on earlier works that identified personality characteristics associated with creativity. Elementary school teachers were then asked to rate their favorite and least favorite students based on these characteristics, there was a significant difference between the teachers' judgments of their favorite and least favorite students on these measures. Their favorite students tended to have profiles consistent with characteristics that were least descriptive of creative children. To summarize:

- Their *least* favorite students had profiles which were more consistent with characteristics typical of *creative* children.
- The teachers favored the students who exhibited fewer "creative" traits.
- Judgments for the favorite student were negatively correlated with creativity; judgments for the least favorite student were positively correlated with creativity.

A second study explored the conflict between the results of the first study and teachers' self-reports that they enjoy working with creative children. Teachers' concepts of creativity were different from concepts of researchers. The table below (Table 2) compares the difference in concepts about creativity between teachers and researchers.

In 2010, Karwowski, studied more than 600 Polish teachers to identify personality characteristics of students whom teachers perceive to be creative and to the characteristics of good students. She found that creative students

Table 2. The discrepancy between teachers' and researchers' concepts of creativity

Teacher Creativity Concepts	Researcher Creativity Concepts
Sincere	Spontaneous rules
Responsible	Impulsive
Good-Natured	Non-conformist
Reliable	Tries the impossible
Logical	Emotional

were perceived as more dynamic, intellectual, and excitable and less agreeable and conscientious than "good" students. The idea that the perceived profile of creative students is significantly different from "good" is a concern. If creativity is to be supported in a classroom the idea that actions or thinking creatively are "bad" can negatively impact development and sustainability of this critical attribute.

Teachers serve as models of thinking and set expectations of behavior in their classrooms and it is quite possible that those same teachers are extinguishing creative behaviors. One may see the similarity to what is called Stockholm syndrome, a psychological response wherein a captive begins to identify closely with his or her captors, as well as with their agenda and demands. Though an extreme example, the time spent being stopped from outside-the-box thinking must have some effect on a person's thinking and beliefs about their thinking and what is acceptable. Educator, Maya Angelou, once said, "We are all creative, but by the time we are three or four years old, someone has knocked the creativity out of us. Some people shut up the kids who start to tell stories. Kids dance in their cribs, but someone will insist they sit still. By the time the creative people are ten or twelve, they want to be like everyone else" (Angelou, n.d.).

High Stakes Accountability and Creativity

The emphasis on standardized testing has intensified in recent decades as elected officials, business leaders, and others have fostered the idea that the U.S. economy will decline unless student achievement and school progress is increasingly monitored through testing (Neill, 2009). Baker (2011) refutes the proposition that higher test scores lead to long-term economic success. In fact, there is a widely-held premise that good schools are equated with good tests scores, and as a result, yields a better economy. Baker (2010) looked at high school students' scores from the First International Mathematics Study (FIMS) test in 1964 and its impact on how competitive the nation's results were 40 years later. Astoundingly, the lower a country's test scores, the stronger its economy was 40 years later. The same held true for schools with high test scores yielding negative effects on seven different measures of economic success. Some schools will try anything to raise test scores which leads to a tunnel vision of teaching to the test and, thus builds a lower set of student skills of rote memorization of what will be tested. Baker (2011) posits, "Is this just like the *flat earth theory* in that it seems like a good idea but without the verification of assumption?" Yet, schools continue in our attempt to raise test scores and prove that our schools are producing successful students, perhaps not with 21st Century qualities and capabilities that society needs.

Opponents of the current accountability system are concerned about how this educational environment influences definitions of academic success; but a new issue has evolved from popular media sources like Newsweek, NPR, Facebook, and Twitter and reports from international agencies like the National Advisory Committee on Creative and Cultural Education (Robinson, 1999), about the declining indicators of creativity in students. The concerns in today's society demand creative and novel resolutions, which require creative thinking and problem solving (Saracho, 2002). The generation of new and valuable ideas is a core component in the ability of individuals and groups both to respond adaptively to change and to envision and bring about change (Runco 2006). As such, creativity is clearly of central importance to human, social, and economic development.

Already existing and validated measures of creative thinking include the *Torrance Tests of Creative Thinking* (TTCT), which is the most widely used test of this kind. These instruments are generally used for identification of the creatively gifted and as a part of gifted matrices in states and districts in the USA and focus on divergent thinking. The TTCT was developed in 1966 and renormed five times. The total sample for all six normative samples includes 272,599 kindergarten through 12th grade students and adults. Analysis of the normative data showed that creative thinking scores remained static or decreased, starting at sixth grade. Results also indicated that since 1990, even as IQ scores have risen, creative thinking scores have significantly decreased. The decrease for kindergartners through third graders was the most significant (Kim, 2011). Adults' accomplishments are linked far more strongly to their creativity than their IQ. It's ironic that even as children are taught the accomplishments of the world's most innovative minds, their own creativity is being squelched (Olien, 2013).

Issues, Controversies, and Problems: Input Versus Outcome

As demands for creativity increase from business leaders (See Figure 1), there is evidence that creativity is decreasing in the United States and other populations. Speculation that the current accountability and requirements for academic success affect the development of creative thinking may be a concern for the future. Bond (2005) reports that a recurring criticism of tests used in high-stakes decision-making is that they distort instruction and force teachers to "teach to the test." The public pressure on students, teachers, principals, and school superintendents to raise scores on high-stakes tests is tremendous, and the temptation to tailor and restrict instruction to only that which will be tested is almost irresistible (Bond, 2005). Few would argue that this accountability system has influenced instructional approaches and reward systems in classrooms, yet little research on the relationship of high stakes tests and creative thinking is available.

Standardized testing limits teachers in improving instruction and the resulting limited instruction takes away from enrichment activities to cover the explicit curriculum and teach test-taking skills. Teachers tend to follow a general pattern to teach only on what the children will be tested. In a

Figure 1. The truth about standardized assessment and the workplace needs
Mike Keefe "Standardized Tests" 01/14/2015 (138693)

study that examined the extent to which math and science teachers regarded standardized tests and focused on creativity in their teaching, all the teachers admitted that the tests represent low levels of thinking. "The test is typically the floor of learning", (p. 44) stated an Algebra teacher (Carroll, 2013). Even if children are lucky enough to have a teacher receptive to their ideas, standardized testing and other programs like No Child Left Behind and Race to the Top (a program whose very designation is opposed to nonlinear creative thinking) make sure children's minds are not on the "wrong" path, the path that supports creative thinking (Olien, 2013).

Weingarten (2013) said that educators should reclaim the promise of public education. She indicated that parents increasingly want change, especially changes in existing policies that they believe hurt their schools and the students. In fact, the majority of parents vehemently reject the "austerity-driven policies gutting schools including over testing and cutbacks in art, music, library and physical education" (p. 1). Nevertheless, a 2013 PDK/Gallup survey found that 74% of the American public said that it is extremely or very important to gauge how their children are doing in school (Maxwell, 2013).

Teacher Preparation and Creativity

It is an accepted practice in the United States to select students for college based on tests like the Scholastic Assessment (SAT) and the American College Test (ACT) which have math and verbal sections but do not have a spatial or other critical thinking sections. Techers may be essentially misidentifying a lot of talented students who are not as math and verbal oriented (Wai, 2012). Ironically, these tests are also used for admission criteria in most teacher education programs in the United States.

The mystery is why these tests are used to determine the potential teaching ability for admissions to teacher training programs at all. SAT the test should primarily be useful as an indicator of academic preparation (US Department of Education, 2012). The ACT is an achievement test, measuring what a student has learned in school (Coy, 2013). An even more disturbing fact is the state of Florida in the U.S. started awarding pay bonuses to teachers based on their ACT and SAT scores. The 2-year-old program rewards teachers based partly on if they had SAT or ACT exam scores in the top 20 percent the year they took them, even if that was decades ago. Experienced teachers also need a "highly effective" evaluation to earn the money, though first-year instructors can receive it solely based on test scores (Postal, 2017). Teachers are being rewarded for old scores that measure what they learned in high school and a predictive measure of academic success in their college careers.

Are there relationships between ACT/SAT tests and creativity? One study (Blake, McCarthy & Krause, 2014) implemented to determine if there is a relationship between creativity and high stakes college admission tests among teacher education students was conducted in 2014. The participant sample was closely matched to the representative sample of the teaching population in the United States: mostly white females coming from middle and upper-middle class environments. Epstein's Creativity Inventory was administered and scores compared to ACT/SAT scores. Epstein creativity skill areas include a) Capturing - related to preserving new ideas as they occur; b) Challenging - taking on difficult tasks; c) Broadening - seeking knowledge and skills outside one's current areas of expertise; and d) Surrounding - seeking out new stimuli or combinations of stimuli. Findings from this study include:

- A significant negative correlation between the SAT and the creativity Capturing category (ability to accept and preserve new ideas).
- No relationship between SAT scores and total creativity scores.
- None of the creativity variables were significant predictors of SAT scores.
- Low scorers on ACT had higher creativity scores.

Disconnect between tests like the ACT and SAT and the expectations of future global leaders seems like an issue that needs rethinking for our teachers and students. Admissions to teacher training programs based on these types of tests seem inappropriate if teacher training programs are seeking professionals who need to understand the concept of creativity. Teachers entering the workforce can no longer rely on a limited set of behaviors to insure academic success for students.

SOLUTIONS AND RECOMMENDATIONS: TEACHER PREPARATION

The real discord at hand is that are educators are not testing the traits that they value- those traits that are essential in the 21st century. This supports a recommendation for an overhaul of the accountability system in schools. The need to value traits that develop and support creativity is essential for countries to thrive in the future economic and employment environment. If educators truly value these skills, schools must adapt the accountability system to address the demand of the future, not the expectations of the past.

The admissions to and training in teacher preparation programs require major change if teachers are to provide support for all students and specifically creative students to develop and thrive in the demands of the creative era. If the premise that most people start with creativity potential, then teachers need to be trained to intentionally provide instructional experiences that allow students to reach their creative potential. The instructional practice would need to better reflect capturing, challenging, broadening and surrounding as identified by Epstein and others as important skills for creativity.

FUTURE RESEARCH DIRECTIONS

It is evident there is much opportunity to research how teacher preparation programs prepare teachers to interact with and support creative students. It is a concern that there are studies that indicate teachers may be biased against creative students in the classroom, despite reports that suggest teachers find creativity to be very important. Future research in this area should further investigate the discrepancies between teachers' reported beliefs about creativity and their documented actions to support creative students in the classroom. Further, the strong focus on standardized testing in current education system needs to be intensely re-examined. If the types of thinking represented on most standardized tests is considered the gold standard by which one we measure success in the field of education, then it follows that the processes that lead to those types of thinking are the goal of teaching. If these types of thinking stand in opposition to creativity then it is foolish to believe that creativity will emerge and flourish under such conditions.

CONCLUSION

This conflicting paradigm of demands for success in the global community and the measures of academic achievement in many schools seems counterproductive, at best, for the millions of students coming through the educational systems. Unfortunately, many educational systems are built on the idea that everybody's mind works in a similar way. Teachers claim to support creativity but the interactions in classrooms seem to erode creative thinking. The trend of teaching test taking skills and specific test driven content in classrooms across twelve years of formal schooling may affect the development and sustainability of creative thinking. Evidence indicates that the adoption of creative thinking models is possible at almost any age, especially when paying additional attention to pedagogic methods and tools that allow demolishing the walls erected by creativity inhibitors (Prins, 2015). Schools sort for compliant auditory learners. At least two thirds of our young people do not get what they need and deserve from our schools in part because of a narrow pedagogical approach (Wai, 2012). The longer a student stays in our schools the less creative they become. If creativity is considered the new literacy of the 21st century, we are educating people out of their creativity (Robinson, 2007).

The time is here to rethink doublethink as the new era of knowledge evolves. What once was is no more. In the forward Carl Williams writes that creativity cannot thrive in an atmosphere of resistance and rigid adherence to the status quo and the way things were. Educational systems must embrace the change needed to prepare our children for the future.

REFERENCES

Adobe Systems Incorporated. (2013). *The creativity gap. State of Create Study*. Retrieved from http://www.adobe.com/aboutadobe/pressroom/pdfs/Adobe_State_of_Create_Global_Benchmark_Study.pdf

Andreasen, N. C. (2006). *The creative brain: The science of genius*. Penguin Random House.

AngelouM. (n.d.). *AZ Quotes*. Retrieved from http://www.azquotes.com/author/440-Maya_Angelou/tag/creativity

Bachtold, L. (1974). The creative personality and the ideal pupil revisited. *The Journal of Creative Behavior*, 8(1), 47–54. doi:10.1002/j.2162-6057.1974.tb01108.x

Baker, K. (2010). A bad idea: National standards based on test scores. *Journal of Scholarship and Practice*, 7(3), 60–68.

Baker, K. (2011). High Test scores: The wrong road to national economic success. *Kappa Delta Pi Record*, 47(3), 116–120. doi:10.1080/00228958.2011.10516574

Berliner, D. C. (2009). *Poverty and potential: Out-of-school factors and school success*. Education Policy Research Unit.

Blake, S., & Giannangelo, D. (2012). Creativity and Young Children: Review of Literature and Connections to Thinking Processes. In O. Saracho & B.Spodek (Eds.), Contemporary Perspectives on Research in Creativity in Early Childhood Education (pp. 289-312). Charlotte, NC: Information Age Publishing.

Blake, S., McCarthy, C., & Krause, J. (2014). The paradoxical nature of academic measures and creativity. *Creative Education, 5*, 797-802. Published Online June 2014 in SciRes. http://www.scirp.org/journal/ce<ALIGNMENT.qj></ALIGNMENT>10.4236/ce.2014.510092

Bond, L. (2005). *Teaching to the test. Carnegie Foundation for the Advancement of Teaching*. Retrieved from http://www.carnegiefoundation.org

Bronson, P., & Merryman, A. (2010, July 7). The Creativity Crisis. *Newsweek*. Retrieved from www.thedailybeast.com/newsweek/2010/07/10/the-creatvity-crisis.html

Carroll, J.M. (2013). The bringing kids up to level: Are critical thinking and creativity lost in the world of standardized tests? *University of New Orleans Theses and Dissertations*. Paper 1616.

Coy, P. (2013). What's Holding American Students Back? The SAT. *Bloomberg Business Week*. Retrieved from: http://www.businessweek.com/articles/2013-10-03/sat-act-college-admissions-tests-are-holding-american-students-back

Cropley, A. J. (1992). *More ways than one: Fostering creativity*. Norwood, NJ: Ablex.

Cropley, A. J. (2001). *Creativity in education and learning: a guide for teachers and educators*. Sterling, VA: Stylus.

Dettmer, P. (1981). Improving teacher attitudes toward characteristic of the creatively gifted. *Gifted Child Quarterly*, 25(1), 11–16. doi:10.1177/001698628102500103

Einstein, A. (n.d.). *Einstein*. Retrieved https://www.psychologytoday.com/blog/freedom-learn/201107/what-einstein-twain-forty-eight-others-said-about-school

Elmore, T. (2012). How schools today thwart creativity [Blog post]. *Leading the Next Generation*. Retrieved from https://growingleaders.com/blog/how-schools-today-thwart-creativity/

Epstein, R. (1991). Skinner, creativity, and the problem of spontaneous behavior. *Psychological Science*, 6(6), 362–370. doi:10.1111/j.1467-9280.1991.tb00168.x

Epstein, R. (1996). *Cognition, creativity, and behavior: Selected essays.* Westport, CT: Praeger.

Epstein, R. (1999). Generativity theory. In M. A. Runco & S. Pritzker (Eds.), Encyclopedia of Creativity (pp. 759–766). Academic Press.

Epstein, R., Kaminaka, K., Phan, V., & Uda, R. (2013). How is creativity best managed? Some empirical and theoretical guidelines. *Creativity and Innovation Management*, 22(4), 359–374. doi:10.1111/caim.12042

Epstein, R., Schmidt, S. M., & Warfel, R. (2008). Measuring and training creativity competencies: Validation of a new test. *Creativity Research Journal*, 20(1), 7–12. doi:10.1080/10400410701839876

Getzels, J. W., & Jackson, P. W. (1962). *Creativity and intelligence.* New York: Wiley.

Giang, V. (2013). *Our education system is killing creativity.* TED Talk. Retrieved from http://www.businessinsider.com/a-ted-talk-on-how-the-education-systen-is-killing-creativity-2013-1

Jobs, S. (n.d.). *Top 15 quotes on education from Steve Jobs.* Retrieved from https://studentaffairscollective.org/top-15-steve-jobs-quotes-on-education/

Kageyama, N. (2016). Do we have a hidden bias against creative people? *The Creativity Post.* Retrieved from: http://www.bulletproofmusician.com/do-we-have-a-hidden-bias-against-creative-people/

Karwowski, M. (2010). Are creative students really welcome in the classroom? Implicit theories of good and creative student personality among Polish teachers. *Procedia: Social and Behavioral Sciences*, 2(2), 1233–1237. doi:10.1016/j.sbspro.2010.03.179

Kim, K. H. (2011). The creativity crisis: The decrease in creative thinking scores on the Torrance tests of creative thinking. *Creativity Research Journal*, 23(4), 285–295. doi:10.1080/10400419.2011.627805

Master, N. (n.d.). *Education: Average number of Schooling compared.* Retrieved from http://www.nationmaster.com/country-info/stats/Education/Average-years-of-schooling-of-adults

Maxwell, L. A. (2013). Common Core: A puzzle to Public. *Education Week, 33*(2), 1, 20–21.

Meador, K. S. (1992). Emerging rainbows: A review of the literature on creativity. *Journal for the Education of the Gifted, 15*(2), 163–181. doi:10.1177/016235329201500205

Myers, R. E., & Torrance, E. P. (1961). Can teachers encourage creative thinking? *Educational Leadership, 19*, 156–159.

Neill, M. (2009). A child is not a test score. Assessment as a civil rights issue. *Root and Branch.* Retrieved from http://www.fairtest.org/files/

Olien, J. (2013, December). *Inside the box: People don't like creativity.* Retrieved from http://www.slate.com/articles/health_and_science/science/2013/12/creativity_is_rejected_teachers_and_bosses_don_t_value_out_of_the_box_thinking.html

Orwell, G. (1949). *Nineteen Eighty-Four.* London: Martin Secker & Warburg Ltd.

Postal, L. (2017, March 12). About 7,200 teachers win "best brightest" bonuses this year. *Orlando Sentinel.*

Prins, G. (2015). Does our education system kill creativity? In *Imagine the Impossible. Practical Manual for Innovation.* Linked In. Retrieved from https://www.linkedin.com/pulse/does-our-education-system-kill-creativity-imagine-impossible-prins

Reavis, G. (1940). *Animal School.* Peterborough, NH: Crystal Springs Books. Retrieved from http://agsc.tamu.edu/384/AnimalSchool.pdf

Robinson, K. (1999). *All our futures: Creativity, culture and education. A report to the Department of Education and Employment, Department for Culture, Media, and Sport.* London: Department for Education and Employment.

Robinson, K. (2007). *Do schools kill creativity?* TED talk. Retrieved from https://www.ted.com/talks/ken_robinson_says_schools_kill_creativity

Runco, M. A. (2004). Creativity. *Annual Review of Psychology, 55*(1), 657–687. doi:10.1146/annurev.psych.55.090902.141502 PMID:14744230

Runco, M. A. (2006). The development of children's creativity. In B. Spodek & N. Saracho (Eds.), *Handbook of the research on the education of young children* (pp. 121–131). Mahwah, NJ: Erlbaum.

Saracho, O. N. (2002). Young childrens creativity and pretend play. *Early Child Development and Care, 172*(5), 431–438. doi:10.1080/03004430214553

Shah, A. (2013). 21st century skills, education & competitiveness: A resource and policy guide. Washington, DC: Partnership for 21st Century Skills.

ShawG. B. (n.d.). *Quotes about education.* Retrieved from http://ireland-calling.com/george-bernard-shaw-quotes-education/

Stone, B. G. (1980). Relationship between creativity and classroom behavior. *Psychology in the Schools, 17*(1), 106–108. doi:10.1002/1520-6807(198001)17:1<106::AID-PITS2310170119>3.0.CO;2-R

Torrance, E. P. (1963). The creative personality and the ideal pupil. *Teachers College Record, 65,* 220–226.

US Department of Education. (2012). *The Condition of Education 2012: A Report from Institute of Educational Sciences.* Washington, DC: National Center for Educational Statistics.

Wai, J. (2012). *The educational world is flat.* A conversation with Tom Vander Ark. The Creative Post. Retrieved from http://www.creativitypost.com/education/the_educational_world_is_flat

Weingarten, R. (2013). Reclaiming the promise of public education. *American Educator, 37*(3), 1–3.

Westby, E. L., & Dawson, V. L. (1995). Creativity: Asset or burden in the classroom? *Creativity Research Journal, 8*(1). Retrieved from http://www.tandfonline.com/doi/abs/10.1207/s15326934crj0801_1

Zhou, J. (2012). Doublethink: The creativity-testing conflict. *Education Week.* Retrieved from http://zhaolearning.com/2012/08/16/doublethink-the-creativity-testing-conflict/

Zhou, J., Shen, J., Wang, X., Neber, H., & Johji, I. (2013). A cross-cultural comparison: Teachers conceptualizations of creativity. *Creativity Research Journal, 25*(3), 239–247. doi:10.1080/10400419.2012.730006

Chapter 4
The Science of Creativity

ABSTRACT

There is a common misconception that only certain individuals "have what it takes" to be creative and the rest of us are destined to lack creativity. However, a review of the relevant neurological and cognitive literatures suggests otherwise- that creative thinking is rooted in everyday cognitive mechanisms and processes. This chapter provides an overview of the neurological and cognitive bases of creativity, with a focus on the role of the pre-frontal cortex and inhibitory control in the creative process. The implication of the findings discussed in this chapter is that, although some people engage in more creative processes than others, we are all equipped with a brain that is complex enough for us to think creatively.

INTRODUCTION: CREATIVITY AND THE INDIVIDUAL

The idea that some people are creative and some people are not comes from at least three sources: (1) the admiration of the highly creative in our society, (2) daily life experiences, and (3) labeling certain fields as creative and others as non-creative. Consider for a moment that you conduct an Internet search for creative people: you will likely turn up websites about artists, authors, musicians and inventors and encounter various websites about people such as Leonardo da Vinci, Maya Angelou, Wolfgang Amadeus Mozart, and Albert Einstein. You will likely find information about their greatest works, their life experiences and typical daily habits that differentiate them from other, "less creative," people. To be sure, there is something special about these

DOI: 10.4018/978-1-5225-4952-9.ch004

Copyright © 2018, IGI Global. Copying or distributing in print or electronic forms without written permission of IGI Global is prohibited.

individuals and their creative works that should be admired. It is, indeed, common to think that such individuals were born with a gift that others could never possess or that the structure of their brains or genetic make-up are vastly different from the "average" person.

Although odds are that most of us have never met (or at least become intimately close to) famously creative individuals such as those mentioned above, we all know people in our every day lives who we consider to be more creative, and unique, than others. To illustrate this, let us consider an everyday example that has become a social media phenomenon- Pinterest (https://www.pinterest.com/). As many of us can attest, there is a difference between generating an idea to post on Pinterest, appreciating an idea on Pinterest, and successfully carrying out a Pinterest project. The very popularity of "Pinterest Fails" further perpetuates that some people are capable of creative endeavors and some are not. This is, in fact, a rather common misconception suggesting that there are those that are creative and those who are not with no possibility of change (Plucker, Beghetto & Dow, 2004; Treffinger, Isaksen, & Dorval, 1996).

To further perpetuate the idea that only certain individuals "have what it takes" to be creative, Carson (2010) notes that we often appreciate creativity in the arts and sciences (e.g., artists, designers, authors, inventors) and neglect the creativity involved in other fields (e.g., project management, education, stock trading, etc.). We would be remiss to discuss creativity only as it relates to the arts and sciences when, in fact, elements of creativity are a part of nearly everything humans do on a daily basis. Specifically, creativity is highly involved in the world of business where, at a minimum "you need to find creative ways to cut costs while maintaining quality, and provide an innovative product or service"(Carson, 2010, pg. 8). Even when creativity is discussed in the business world there is still a strong focus on those individuals considered to be creative (e.g., Steve Jobs) as compared to those who are not. This, again, further perpetuates the notion that some people "have it" and some people do not.

Our daily lives and experiences would certainly lead us to believe that creativity is an elusive trait that can only be possessed by individuals with certain brain characteristics and optimal genetics. Accordingly, those in search of defining the creativity "it" factor often turn to neuroscience and genetics to explain differences in the brains of those who are considered creative as compared to those who are not. It is tempting to think that there is "a creativity gene that makes the human species the most innovative one on the planet, or that genetic differences between people might make one person more creative than another" (Sawyer, 2012, pg. 157). In fact, scientists have yet to isolate a "creativity gene," but rather cite a variety of evidence to support that creativity is based in everyday cognitive processes (Sawyer, 2012).

Objectives

The purpose of this chapter is to explore what conclusions can be drawn from neuroscience and cognitive studies about the creative brain. That is, what neurological and cognitive mechanisms and processes are most related to creativity in individuals? Is there evidence to support that some people have the genetic and neurological make up that pre-destine them to be creative individuals or does available evidence suggest that creativity is rooted in everyday cognitive processes? First we will begin with a brief tour of the parts of the brain and their corresponding functions, then we will discuss in more detail the portions of the brain believed to be most related to creativity, and finally we will consider the mental processes associated with creative thought.

BACKGROUND: HOW WE LEARN

A lot of people in our industry haven't had very diverse experiences. So they don't have enough dots to connect, and they end up with very linear solutions - Steve Jobs (1996)

The human brain is considered to be large, especially when compared to other mammals, and is considerably larger than our earliest human predecessors (Carlsson, 2014; Navarrete, van Schaik & Isler, 2011). As our brains have expanded in size over time, so to has our capacity to engage in more complex thinking, planning and acting- including the complex thinking that is associated with creativity (Carlsson, 2014). In addition to physiological changes, modifications in our environments and living conditions over time have allowed humans, as a species, to be less preoccupied with survival and, therefore, has freed up more time and resources to being creative (Carson, 2010). Not only has the human brain evolved over time, but also advances in medical technology have allowed us to observe what is happening inside people's heads. Advances in brain imaging, for example, have allowed scientists to see what is happening in the brain while people are engage in various cognitive tasks (Sawyer, 2012). This research is based on the assumption that what can be seen happening in the brain while someone engages in a certain processing activity reflects the brain functions required to carry out such processes. In other words, "the fundamental assumption guiding all cognitive neuroscience is that all of our sensations, thoughts and mental processing are based in the biological brain, and that when we have a subjective experience of a mental event, the neuronal activity of the brain that occurs at the same time is responsible for that experience" (Sawyer, 2012, pg. 185).

Even simple activities and behaviors we can observe with the naked eye require a great deal of complex interactions in the brain. The brain has a very large number of nerve cells (100 billion neurons) that can form nearly infinite connections with other neurons (more than 100 trillion possible connections) (Addis, Wong, & Schacter, 2007 as cited in Carson, 2010). Learning involves creating connections between neurons, some of which are accessed more than others (Carson, 2010). For example, we learn through experience that snow is cold- the more experience we have with this the stronger the connections are in our brains that link snow to cold. A child who spent their entire childhood in California, for example, would not have as strong of a connection between snow and cold as a child growing up in Alaska. Because the child in Alaska has more frequent experience connecting snow and cold, the link between them in the brain is stronger and anytime the child thinks "snow," then "cold" is automatically, and immediately, activated. For the child in California it is entirely possible that "cold" is also activated when they think about "snow," but it will be more distantly related and, therefore, not be as quickly accessed as it would be for the child from Alaska.

Another way to think of it, according to Carson (2010) is that making connections between two pieces of information is akin to building a highway between the two and the more you connect the information the bigger the highway. Imagine that you have a long commute to work and there are two ways you can go- two "links" between home and work- one that you have used every day for the last two years and one that you have only taken twice when your typical route was closed for construction. Both routes are the same number of miles and have similar numbers of curves and turns, but your typical route is a paved, frequently traveled highway and your secondary route consists of less familiar back-roads. On your typical route you are so familiar with the curves and turns that you know where they are- and exactly how long it will take you to maneuver them, whereas you are far less familiar with the intricacies of the second back-road route. Because of your experience and familiarity- you can arrive to work in nearly half the time when you take your typical route than when you take the back-roads, even though the two routes are the same distance. Similarly, more experience connecting two pieces of information in the brain leads to a stronger, faster connection between the two pieces of information.

THE BRAIN AND CREATIVITY: EVIDENCE FROM NEUROSCIENCE

There is no doubt that creativity is dependent on processes and connections generated in the brain. The question is- what brain processes are most related to creative thought and where in the brain do those processes take place? In the following section we will first review the parts of the brain and then focus exclusively on the parts of the brain most related to creativity.

The largest part of the human brain is the cerebrum that is split into two hemispheres (right and left) (Carlsson, 2014; Carson, 2010). Each of the two hemispheres is divided into four lobes that are responsible for various aspects of mental activity (see Figure 1 for diagram): the temporal, parietal, occipital and frontal lobes (Carson, 2010). The temporal lobe is responsible for language comprehension and integrating information into memories. The occipital lobe is responsible for processing visual stimuli. The parietal lobe is responsible for sensory perception and integration as well as spatial skills (Carson, 2010). Finally, the frontal lobe, the largest part of the cerebrum, is responsible for motor movement as well as higher-order skills and cognitive functions such as abstract reasoning, planning and decision-making (Carlsson, 2014; Carson, 2010). Specifically, the prefrontal cortex, a part of the frontal lobe, "represents the neural basis of higher cognitive functions" (Dietrich, 2004, pg. 1012).

The prefrontal cortex (see Figure 2 for a diagram) integrates information within the brain and conducts higher cognitive functions such as abstract thinking, sustained attention, and cognitive flexibility, all of which are related to creativity (Ashby, Valentin & Turken, 2002; Carlsson, Wendt, & Risberg, 2000; Dietrich, 2004; Martindale, 1999; Posner, 1994). The prefrontal cortex is also related to executive control and working memory, the system used to "hold information in temporary storage to complete [complex tasks]" (Baddeley, 1996, pg. 13468). Given the complexity of creative thinking, the role of the prefrontal cortex and higher order processing cannot be overemphasized. Dietrich (2004, pg. 1015) has suggested as least three roles the prefrontal cortex plays in creativity. First, beyond generating connections between neurons, in order for a novel combination of ideas to be complete a

Figure 1. Diagram of the four lobes of the brain

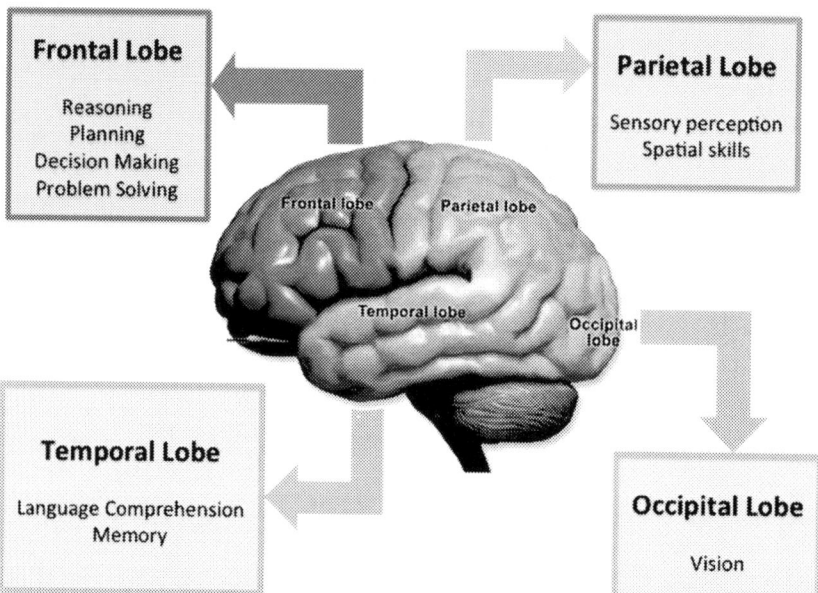

person has to be aware of the novel thought to evaluate it for appropriateness. To become aware of the generation of a creative idea, or novel connections between two mental elements, one must obviously have the to-be-combined elements both in the focus of their attention at the same time (Martindale, 1999; Mendelsohn, 1976). As intuitive as that may seem, it's actually fairly complicated and requires a number of mental processes. For example, one must have the capacity to hold multiple ideas in their attention at the same time (called Working Memory Capacity) and also have the ability to navigate their way among less-familiar connections.

Second, once novel combinations of information have occurred, the prefrontal cortex is responsible for the higher order functions that act on that novel combination. In other words, having a creative thought is one thing while acting on it is another- both requiring processing in the prefrontal cortex. Third, the prefrontal cortex is responsible for the expression of the novel thought. There is a often a great deal of thinking, planning and revising associated with most effectively expressing a creative thought to others. This type of higher-order activity would be dependent upon the prefrontal cortex.

Your brain is continuously learning by generating new connections among neurons, but those connections are only one piece of the puzzle. In order for

Figure 2. Diagram of the location of the prefrontal cortex

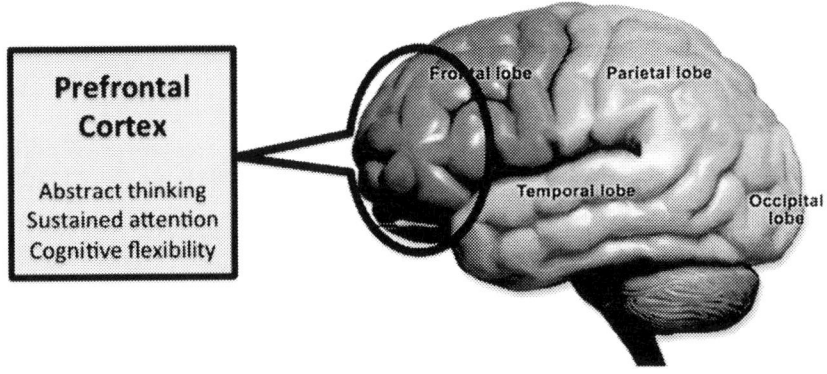

a creative product to be realized, there are multiple higher order functions that have to take place- and those higher order functions are linked to the prefrontal cortex. Creative productions always consist of novel combinations of pre-existing mental elements or the realization of the relationship between previously unassociated mental elements (Martindale, 1999). To continue the highway metaphor- one must either find a novel route to connect home and work, or one must connect home to an entirely new destination that has never been connected before. In the following section, we will consider the role of executive functioning in creativity. Executive functioning is widely accepted as the mechanism responsible for attentional focus- a key feature in creativity.

MEASURING CREATIVITY: ELEMENTS OF PROBLEM SOLVING

Many psychological experimental studies of creativity focus on processes involved in creative problem solving tasks where the most familiar and obvious solutions to a problem will not result in the desired outcome. According to Mayer (1999), "The underlying view is of creativity as cognitive processing: Creativity is best understood by analyzing the cognitive processes of people as they engage in creative thinking on a given creativity problem" (pg. 454). In fact, the relationship between creativity and problem solving has been emphasized for decades (Kaufmann, Helstrup, & Teigen, 1995). Guilford (1977), for example, described creative thinking as a subset of problem solving and emphasizes that the underlying relationship between the two lies in producing novel outcomes (Kaufmann, Helstrup, & Teigen, 1995). How does one arrive at such novel outcomes? As an example, Kaufmann and colleagues (1995) outline a model for creative problem solving that specifies a series of processes involved in creatively solving a problem: understanding the problem, generating ideas, and planning for action. According to Kaufmann et al., (1995), the understanding the problem component involves identifying and analyzing the problem or task to be tackled. The generating ideas and planning for action components involve coming up with a large variety of possible options and solutions to the problem/task and a process of narrowing those options down to those that show the most promise. Through rounds of refinement that continually evaluates and narrows possible solutions, the ideal outcome is a creative or novel solution that has great potential.

Admittedly, the creative problem solving process described above could look similar for any problem solving scenario and not necessarily a task that requires creativity or novel solutions. After all, it is true that in all problem-solving situations, the solver must construct a representation of the problem and then make attempts (some successful, some not) to solve it. What, then, differentiates non-creative problem solving from creative problem solving? A major difference between creative problem solving and non-creative problem solving lies less in the *process* involved in solving the problem and more so in what counts as a solution. According to Wiley & Jarosz (2012b), for a creative problem, "the most dominant solutions or most obvious solution paths will not lead to success. When a person approaches a creative problem, the solution requires either a completely original approach or a novel combination of diverse bits of information through remote associations in memory" (pg. 204). So although the processes involved in creative problem solving can be very similar to non-creative problem solving, the elements and connections lead to a novel solution.

Remote Associates Test (RAT)

There are a number of tasks often used by creative problem solving researchers to measure various aspects of creativity. One particularly prevalent measure of creativity used by psychologists is the Remote Associates Test (RAT) developed by Mednick (1962). In the following section we will give a detailed example of a typical RAT problem intended to be representative of the types of processing that typically occur during creative problem solving tasks, which constitute the basis of claims about the relationship between creativity and executive functioning.

To solve a RAT problem, participants are given three words that appear to be unrelated (e.g., stool, powder and ball) and are asked to determine a fourth word that is related to each of the three given words. In the above example the fourth word that is related to stool, powder, and ball is foot – footstool, foot powder, and football. Some of the examples problems are easier to solve than others. For example, when given the three words falling, actor and dust it is relatively easy to come up with a fourth word- star. On the other hand, when given the words shopping, washer and picture it may take more effort to come up with window as the fourth word.

Part of accounting for the differences in difficulty to solve lies in the processes involved in solving the given item. Generally speaking, the way the process works is that you read one word and many other ideas are automatically generated. For example, if I were to give you the word shopping and ask you what comes to mind you would likely say cart, money, bag, grocery, cashier, etc. These are some examples of the words that are most associated with shopping- the words that will come to mind first. The target of the RAT problem- window- is a more remote associate, meaning that it doesn't come to mind as quickly as some of the more immediate associates (e.g., cart). The process repeats for each of the three words for each RAT problem and the goal is to come up with the one remotely associated word that connects all three given words.

In Figure 3 (a diagram of the processes associated with RAT problem solving), a person is given the three words in the example above (shopping, washer and picture) and expected to find a word that relates the three to each other. As seen in the figure, each word has a variety of other words associated with it, some are more frequently and more strongly associated, whereas others are more remotely associated. Examples of words that are strongly associated with shopping are cart and money, slightly less strongly associated might words such as bag and grocery. The more remotely associated the words in the figure, the longer the connecting arrow. As seen in the figure, for all three words (shopping, washer and picture) window is only remotely associated. This reinforces the goal of a RAT problem- to find a word that is a remote associate (window) for all three of the provided words (shopping, washer, and picture).

The RAT problem above demonstrates an example of the types of processing involved in creative problem solving. The role of the prefrontal cortex in such creative tasks as solving RAT problems cannot be over emphasized. Each of

Figure 3. Diagram of RAT creative problem solving example

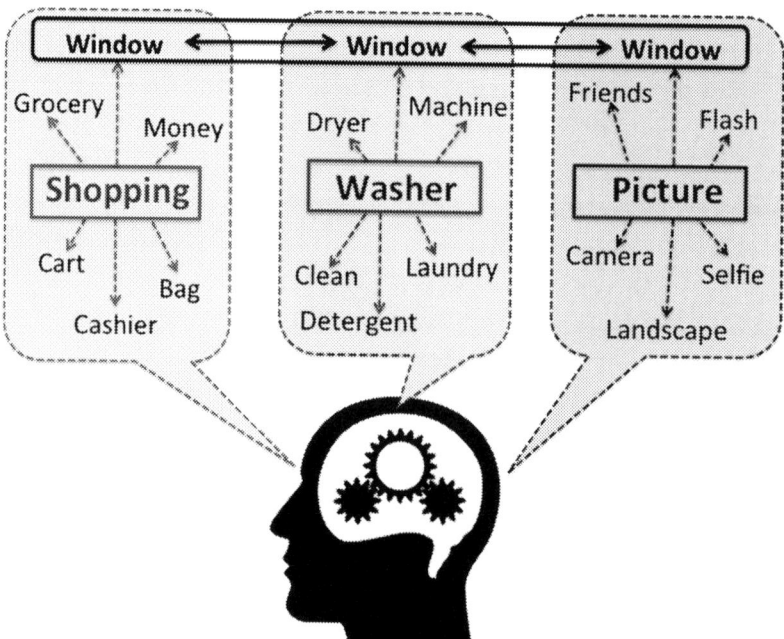

the processes used in creative problem solving would depend on the higher-order functions of the prefrontal cortex that were described in the previous Parts of the Brain section of this chapter. A particularly important process believed to rely on prefrontal cortex activation, executive functioning, is especially important to creative problem solving. More specifically, executive functioning, a name for the various processes believed to be responsible for aspects of mental control, is widely accepted as the mechanism responsible for attentional focus- a key feature in creativity that will be discussed in more detail in the next section of this chapter.

CREATIVITY AND EXECUTIVE FUNCTIONING: THE GOLDILOCKS PARADOX

There is a great deal of evidence to support that there is a relationship between various aspects of executive functioning and creativity (Ansburg & Hill, 2003; Barr, Pennycook, Stolz, & Fugelsang, 2015; Beaty, Silvia, Nusbaum, Jauk, & Benedek, 2014; Benedek, Jauk, Sommer, Arendasy & Neubauer, 2014;

Carson, Peterson, & Higgins, 2003; Cassotti, Agogué, Camarda, Houdé, & Borst, 2016; Cheng, He, Jia, & Runco, 2016; Edl, Benedek, Papousek, Weiss, & Fink, 2014; Jarosz, Colflesh & Wiley, 2012; Radel, Davranche, Fournier & Dietrich, 2015). The nature of the relationship, however, is less clear. Some studies emphasize that lower levels of executive functioning is related to creativity (e.g., Jarosz, Colflesh & Wiley, 2012; Radel, Davranche, Fournier & Dietrich, 2015) while others suggest that higher levels of executive functioning is related to creativity (e.g., Benedek, et al., 2014; Cassotti, et al., 2016, Edl et al., 2014). Still others claim that *both* high and low levels of executive functioning are related to creativity (Cheng et al., 2016) and others emphasize the importance of flexibility between high and low levels of executive functioning is the key (Zabelina & Robinson, 2010). In order to better understand the arguments put forth by both sides (higher executive vs. lower executive) first let us consider what potential roles executive functioning could play in creative problem solving.

Creativity and Connections

Generally speaking, the way the brain works is through spreading activation- information is encoded as units, connections are made between the units, and those connections that are made more often, or are more strongly related, have a higher level of activation than those more distantly related (Anderson, 1983). Recall the earlier description of connecting neurons and highways- the more frequent connections the more accessible the highway or link between two locations. Because these more frequent connections have a higher activation in the brain (meaning they are more easily accessible)- attention during any type of problem solving will likely be focused on the more familiar connections and dominant connections (Wiley & Jarosz, 2012a). In other words, when solving problems, attention is likely to be focused on the most accessible information (the most familiar highway) and, therefore, restrict access to the less accessible/familiar information that would be important to creating new connections for creative solutions. When solving non-creative problems, where the most obvious and direct solution is the goal, the ability to screen out excess or less familiar information could be an asset. Conversely, when solving creative problems, where the most obvious and direction solution is *NOT* the goal a novel solution could be hindered by a failure to consider the less familiar information that is outside of one's attentional focus.

This is at the very crux of the lower vs. higher executive functioning debate. On the one hand, higher executive functioning would include an increased ability to keep relevant information in your attentional focus, which would increase the likelihood of making connections among such information- and, therefore, be related to high levels of creativity. On the other hand, because our brain works in a way that the most familiar and dominant concepts are activated more quickly and strongly than more remotely related concepts, a high level of attentional focus would likely hinder creativity because the natural focus would be on concepts most familiar and closely related- the opposite of generating novel connections.

Inhibitory Control

One thing about the processes involved in problem solving is certain- when working on a task there are many activated concepts in our brain that are competing for our attention at any given movement (Mendelsohn, 1976 as cited in Ansburg & Hill 2003). Fortunately, the brain has a way to focus on relevant information and screen out the irrelevant. Inhibitory control, sometimes referred to as latent inhibition, is the brain's capacity to screen out information deemed irrelevant- a way to focus attention on those aspects that are most relevant to the task at hand (Lubow, 1989 as cited in Carson, Peterson & Higgins, 2003; Sharma & Babu, 2017). In other words, inhibition is a mechanism responsible for narrowing the focus of attentional resources around specific, goal-related, information (Radel, Davranche, Fournier & Dietrich, 2015). Those who are high in inhibition are adept at focusing on the information most directly related to a task, and ignoring "distractor" information. On the other hand, "when inhibitory control is inefficient, a broader range of information will penetrate working memory causing the apparition of less relevant thoughts" (Radel et al., 2015, pg. 111).

One of the most common experimental methods for measuring inhibitory control is a Stroop task (Stroop, 1935). In order to highlight the processes involved in inhibitory control let us consider an example of a Stroop task. The most common example involves showing participants a series of color words, for example, red. The color of font the word is printed in is different for different trials. For example sometimes the word red would be printed in red ink and sometimes the word red would be printed in blue ink. One task is for you to say the ink color the words are printed in and the time you take to respond is timed. The Stroop effect occurs when it takes you longer to say what color a word is printed in when the ink is a different color than the concept represented (e.g., the word red printed in blue ink) than it does to say what color a word is when the ink color and represented concept match (e.g., the word red printed in red ink). There are multiple explanations for this phenomena, but inhibitory control definitely plays a role- because it takes less time to read the word than to identify the color of the ink, when the two don't match (i.e., the word red printed in blue ink) your brain has to inhibit the most dominant response- the word itself- and respond with the color of the ink. This example illustrates the crux of inhibitory control- having to inhibit the most dominant response that is more quickly activated in your brain and, instead, focus on a less dominant response.

Creativity and Inhibitory Control

One goal of inhibitory control is to filter which information is more relevant and which is less relevant, regardless of speed and strength of activation in the brain. What, then, is optimal for creativity- greater or lesser degrees of control? After all, there has to be some degree of inhibitory control at work or else we would have so much information equally activated at once that we would not have enough resources left over to engage in higher-order processes. With no inhibitory control, it is possible that our system would be overloaded with information and our all of our resources would be occupied storing information. Conversely, if our inhibitory control were too strict, we would not have the opportunity to make connections between more remote associates because our attention would be narrowed down to only a few pieces of information, likely that which is the most strongly activated or familiar to us. It seems, then, that we are stuck in a Goldilocks paradox where too much or too little inhibitory control can be potentially detrimental to creativity. The implication of such a system would suggest the possibility of a "just right" level of inhibitory control that would allow for the novel associations required for creative processing, but focuses our attention only on those connections that are most relevant. The remainder of this section will consider the evidence to support the high inhibition, low inhibition and "just right" accounts of the relationship between inhibition and creativity.

First, let us consider the argument that increased inhibitory control is important to creativity. For one thing, humans have a limited working memory capacity and the brain can only engage in higher-order processing on so much information at once. In other words, the more information that is being held in working memory, the less processing capacity is available to conduct higher-order functions on that information (Ansburg & Hill, 2003). From this perspective, the fewer items in working memory the greater the capacity to engage in more complex processing activities- which could result in a higher likelihood for creative outcomes.

There is, indeed, empirical support for a relationship between greater inhibitory control and higher levels of creativity. For example, Benedek, Franz, Heene & Neubauer (2012) found a positive relationship between inhibition (measured using a random motor generation test) and creativity as measured through multiple divergent thinking tests. Later, Benedek et al., 2014 also found a positive relationship between inhibition (measured through Stroop tasks) and creativity measured through divergent thinking tasks. Further, Edl et al., (2014) found a positive relationship between performance on Stroop tasks and creativity measured through the Torrance Tests of Creative Thinking (Torrance, 1966). In addition, Beaty et al., (2014) found that individual differences in executive functioning (measured using verbal fluency and paper folding tasks) predicted creativity (measured using divergent thinking tasks).

Second, let us consider the argument that decreased inhibitory control is important to creativity. Based on what we know about creativity requiring novel connections, it stands to reason that being overly focused on the most dominant information in memory, and ignoring the less-related, or more remote information, would restrict creative abilities. In essence, "too much focus or attentional control may limit creative problem solving- it may limit the scope of solutions that are explored..." (Wiley & Jarosz, 2012a, pg. 260)

There is a good deal of empirical evidence to support the notion that reduced attentional control is related to creative thinking. For example, a meta-analysis investigating the relationship between latent inhibition and creativity that demonstrated a relationship between different indicators of creativity or creative achievement and reduced latent inhibition was conducted by Carson, Peterson, & Higgins (2003). Further, a series of studies conducted by Radel, Davaranche, Fournier, & Dietrich (2015) found that inhibition affects some types of the creative processes. In addition, a study conducted by Jarosz, Colflesh & Wiley (2012) demonstrated that participants with moderate alcohol intoxication outscored their sober comparison condition counterparts on creative problem solving tasks. The authors explained this effect in terms of alcohol's impact on one's ability to control their attention.

In other words, while moderately intoxicated, participants were less able to screen out peripheral information (inhibition) and, therefore, performed better on creative tasks.

SOLUTIONS AND RECOMMENDATIONS

How shall we explain contradictory evidence that suggests both that increased *and* decreased inhibitory control is related to creativity? It seems unlikely, if not impossible, that both are true. Interestingly, there are researchers who provide explanations for how both sets of findings could, in fact, be true. Namely, some researchers subscribe to the notion that creative thought actually includes some processes that would benefit from reduced inhibition and some processes that would benefit from greater inhibitory control. For example, Cheng et al., (2016) conducted an experiment where they measured inhibition using a random motor generator test and creativity using the Creative Problem Finding Test (Hu, Shi, Han, Wang & Adey, 2010). Their results indicated an interaction such that low inhibition was beneficial for originality in the early stages of problem solving, but higher inhibitory control was more beneficial later in the creative process. In addition, Zabelina & Robinson (2010) conducted an experiment motivated by the possibility that "creative individuals are better able to modulate the functioning of their cognitive control system in a context-sensitive manner" (pg. 136). Their results supported that participants who scored higher on measures of creativity demonstrated more flexible cognitive control. In other words, participants who scored higher on creativity tasks demonstrated more control over their cognitive processes (including inhibition) and fluctuated their processes based on the context of the to-be-solved task.

Results of both of the experiments described above suggest that creativity is neither dependent on high or low inhibitory control, but rather the ability to adapt inhibitory control based on task-specific features. Indeed, both accounts seem to bring together the seemingly contradictory findings that both high and low inhibitory control is related to creativity. Rather than being a "just right" account of inhibition, research indicates that the ability to fluctuate levels of inhibitory control based on task demands is likely to be the mechanism behind optimal creative thought.

FUTURE DIRECTIONS AND DIRECTIONS

Although further investigation is needed regarding the Goldilocks paradox, the fact that creativity is rooted in everyday mental processes is promising for the presence of creativity in the workplace. If, in fact, creativity is not some elusive gene that belongs only to the chosen few- then it can be fostered and nurtured both by individual practices as well as elements of the environment. This supports evidence from previous chapters suggesting that creativity can be nurtured (or hindered) under the right conditions. Leaders in the work place should seek to incorporate elements that foster the kinds of thinking and processing that is beneficial for creativity. The final chapter in this book (chapter 6) highlights elements of the work place that can benefit creativity.

Individuals in the work force should engage in tasks that encourage the generation of novel associations between information and increase cognitive flexibility. There is evidence to support multiple methods for increasing cognitive flexibility. For example, research supports a link between meditation and cognitive flexibility (Moore & Malinowski, 2009; Müller, Gerasimova, & Ritter, 2016). There is also evidence to support that physical exercise, specifically running, is related to improved cognitive flexibility (Brockett, LaMarca, & Gould, 2015). Perhaps the most exciting news is that researchers have found that engaging in 2-3 weeks of recreational travel shows an increase in cognitive flexibility upon return to work (de Bloom, Ritter, Kühnel, Reinders & Geurts, 2014).

CONCLUSION

This chapter investigated the following questions: 1) what neurological and cognitive mechanisms and processes are most related to creativity in individuals, and 2) Is there evidence to support that some people have the genetic and neurological make up that pre-destine them to be creative individuals or does available evidence suggest that creativity is rooted in everyday cognitive processes? The research summarized in this chapter leads to the conclusions that creativity is the result of: 1) higher-order processes that occur in the frontal lobe (specifically the prefrontal cortex), 2) relying on certain executive functions (e.g., inhibitory control) to guide attentional focus 3) generating novel connections between information and ideas that are in working memory. When people are engaged in creative tasks, they use brain regions that are commonly used in a wide range of everyday activities (Sawyer, 2012). This is especially clear based on evidence that the processes involved in non-creative and creative problem solving are similar despite drastically different goals and outcomes (Kaufmann, Helstrup, & Teigen, 1995).

The implication of such findings as those descried in this chapter is that we are all equipped with a brain that is complex enough for us to think creatively. Rather than thinking of creativity as a special and elite gift given only to a select few it is better to think of it on a continuum (Shiu, 2014). In other words, we all have the potential to be creative. Although some realize that potential more fully than others, the necessary elements to support creative thinking are present in all of us. That is not to say that we will each be the next Einstein, as there are many internal and external factors that influence our ability to think creatively, but that each of us has the potential to engage in creative thought on some level.

REFERENCES

Addis, D. R., Wong, A. T., & Schacter, D. L. (2007). Remembering the past and imagining the future: Common and distinct neural substrates during event construction and elaboration. *Neuropsychologia, 45*(7), 1378–1385. doi:10.1016/j.neuropsychologia.2006.10.016 PMID:17126370

Anderson, J. R. (1983). A spreading activation theory of memory. *Journal of Verbal Learning and Verbal Behavior, 22*(3), 261–295. doi:10.1016/S0022-5371(83)90201-3

Ansburg, P. I., & Hill, K. (2003). Creative and analytic thinkers differ in their use of attentional resources. *Personality and Individual Differences, 34*(7), 1141–1152. doi:10.1016/S0191-8869(02)00104-6

Ashby, F. G., Valentin, V. V., & Turken, A. U. (2002). The effects of positive affect and arousal on working memory and executive attention. *Advances in Consciousness Research, 44*, 245-288.

Baddeley, A. (1996). The fractionation of working memory. *Proceedings of the National Academy of Sciences of the United States of America, 93*(24), 13468–13472. doi:10.1073/pnas.93.24.13468 PMID:8942958

Barr, N., Pennycook, G., Stolz, J. A., & Fugelsang, J. A. (2015). Reasoned connections: A dual-process perspective on creative thought. *Thinking & Reasoning, 21*(1), 61–75. doi:10.1080/13546783.2014.895915

Beaty, R. E., Silvia, P. J., Nusbaum, E. C., Jauk, E., & Benedek, M. (2014). The roles of associative and executive processes in creative cognition. *Memory & Cognition, 42*(7), 1186–1197. doi:10.3758/s13421-014-0428-8 PMID:24898118

Benedek, M., Franz, F., Heene, M., & Neubauer, A. C. (2012). Differential effects of cognitive inhibition and intelligence on creativity. *Personality and Individual Differences, 53*(4), 480–485. doi:10.1016/j.paid.2012.04.014 PMID:22945970

Benedek, M., Jauk, E., Sommer, M., Arendasy, M., & Neubauer, A. C. (2014). Intelligence, creativity, and cognitive control: The common and differential involvement of executive functions in intelligence and creativity. *Intelligence, 46*, 73–83. doi:10.1016/j.intell.2014.05.007 PMID:25278640

Brockett, A. T., LaMarca, E. A., & Gould, E. (2015). Physical exercise enhances cognitive flexibility as well as astrocytic and synaptic markers in the medial prefrontal cortex. *PLoS ONE, 10*(5), e0124859. doi:10.1371/journal.pone.0124859 PMID:25938418

Carlsson, I. (2014). Biological and neuropsychological aspects of creativity. In E. Shiu (Ed.), *Creativity research: An inter-disciplinary and multi-disciplinary research handbook* (pp. 51–67). New York: Routledge.

Carlsson, I., Wendt, P. E., & Risberg, J. (2000). On the neurobiology of creativity. Differences in frontal activity between high and low creative subjects. *Neuropsychologia, 38*(6), 873–885. doi:10.1016/S0028-3932(99)00128-1 PMID:10689061

Carson, S. (2010). *Your creative brain: Seven steps to maximize imagination, productivity, and innovation in your life.* John Wiley & Sons.

Carson, S. H., Peterson, J. B., & Higgins, D. M. (2003). Decreased latent inhibition is associated with increased creative achievement in high-functioning individuals. *Personality Processes and Individual Differences, 85*(3), 499–506. PMID:14498785

Cassotti, M., Agogué, M., Camarda, A., Houdé, O., & Borst, G. (2016). Inhibitory control as a core process of creative problem solving and idea generation from childhood to adulthood. *New Directions for Child and Adolescent Development, 2016*(151), 61–72. doi:10.1002/cad.20153 PMID:26994725

Cheng, L., Hu, W., Jia, X., & Runco, M. A. (2016). The different role of cognitive inhibition in early versus late creative problem finding. *Psychology of Aesthetics, Creativity, and the Arts, 10*(1), 32–41. doi:10.1037/aca0000036

de Bloom, J., Ritter, S., Kühnel, J., Reinders, J., & Geurts, S. (2014). Vacation from work: A ticket to creativity?: The effects of recreational travel on cognitive flexibility and originality. *Tourism Management, 44*, 164–171. doi:10.1016/j.tourman.2014.03.013

Dietrich, A. (2004). The cognitive neuroscience of creativity. *Psychonomic Bulletin & Review, 11*(6), 1011–1026. doi:10.3758/BF03196731 PMID:15875970

Edl, S., Benedek, M., Papousek, I., Weiss, E. M., & Fink, A. (2014). Creativity and the Stroop interference effect. *Personality and Individual Differences, 69*, 38–42. doi:10.1016/j.paid.2014.05.009

Guilford, J. P. (1977). *Way beyond the IQ: Guide to improving intelligence and creativity*. Buffalo, NY: Bearly Limited.

Hu, W., Shi, Q. Z., Han, Q., Wang, X., & Adey, P. (2010). Creative scientific problem finding and its developmental trend. *Creativity Research Journal, 22*(1), 46–52. doi:10.1080/10400410903579551

Jarosz, A. F., Colflesh, G. J., & Wiley, J. (2012). Uncorking the muse: Alcohol intoxication facilitates creative problem solving. *Consciousness and Cognition, 21*(1), 487–493. doi:10.1016/j.concog.2012.01.002 PMID:22285424

Jobs, S. (1996). Steve Jobs Interview from Wired. Retrieved from: https://www.wired.com/1996/02/jobs-2/

Kaufmann, G., Helstrup, T., & Teigen, K. H. (Eds.). (1995). *Problem solving and cognitive processes: A festschrift in honour of Kjell Raaheim* (pp. 145–181). Bergen-Sandviken, Norway: Fagbokforlaget Vigmostad & Bjørke AS.

Lubow, R. E. (1989). Latent inhibition and conditioned attention theory. Cambridge, UK: Cambridge University Press. doi:10.1017/CBO9780511529849

Martindale, C. (1999). Biological bases of creativity. In R. J. Sternberg (Ed.), Handbook of Creativity (pp. 137-152). New York, NY: Cambridge.

Mayer, R. E. (1999). 22 Fifty Years of Creativity Research. In R. J. Sternberg (Ed.), Handbook of creativity (pp. 449-460). New York, NY: Cambridge.

Mednick, S. (1962). The associative basis of the creative process. *Psychological Review*, *69*(3), 220–232. doi:10.1037/h0048850 PMID:14472013

Mendelsohn, G. A. (1976). Associative and attentional processes in creative performance. *Journal of Personality*, *44*(2), 341–369. doi:10.1111/j.1467-6494.1976.tb00127.x

Moore, A., & Malinowski, P. (2009). Meditation, mindfulness and cognitive flexibility. *Consciousness and Cognition*, *18*(1), 176–186. doi:10.1016/j.concog.2008.12.008 PMID:19181542

Müller, B. C., Gerasimova, A., & Ritter, S. M. (2016). Concentrative meditation influences creativity by increasing cognitive flexibility. *Psychology of Aesthetics, Creativity, and the Arts*, *10*(3), 278–286. doi:10.1037/a0040335

Navarrete, A. F., van Schaik, C. P., & Isler, K. (2011). Energetics and the evolution of human brain size. *Nature*, *480*(7375), 91–93. doi:10.1038/nature10629 PMID:22080949

Plucker, J. A., Beghetto, R. A., & Dow, G. T. (2004). Why isnt creativity more important to educational psychologists? Potentials, pitfalls, and future directions in creativity research. *Educational Psychologist*, *39*(2), 83–96. doi:10.1207/s15326985ep3902_1

Posner, M. I. (1994). Attention: The mechanisms of consciousness. *Proceedings of the National Academy of Sciences of the United States of America*, *91*(16), 7398–7403. doi:10.1073/pnas.91.16.7398 PMID:8052596

Radel, R., Davranche, K., Fournier, M., & Dietrich, A. (2015). The role of (dis) inhibition in creativity: Decreased inhibition improves idea generation. *Cognition*, *134*, 110–120. doi:10.1016/j.cognition.2014.09.001 PMID:25460384

Sawyer, R. K. (2012). *Explaining creativity: The science of human innovation*. Oxford University Press.

Sharma, S., & Babu, N. (2017). Interplay between Creativity, Executive Function and Working Memory in Middle-Aged and Older Adults. *Creativity Research Journal*, 29(1), 71–77. doi:10.1080/10400419.2017.1263512

Shiu, E. (2014). *Creativity research: An inter-disciplinary and multi-disciplinary research handbook* (Vol. 34). Routledge.

Stroop, J. R. (1935). Studies of interference in serial verbal reactions. *Journal of Experimental Psychology*, 18(6), 643–662. doi:10.1037/h0054651

Torrance, E. P. (1966). *Torrance tests of creative thinking*. Bensenville, IL: Scholastic Testing Service.

Treffinger, D. J., Isaksen, S. G., & Dorval, B. K. (1996). Creative problem solving: An overview. In M. A. Runco (Ed.), *Problem finding, problem solving, and creativity* (pp. 223–235). Norwood, NJ: Ablex.

Wiley, J., & Jarosz, A. F. (2012a). Working memory capacity, attentional focus, and problem solving. *Current Directions in Psychological Science*, 21(4), 258–262. doi:10.1177/0963721412447622

Wiley, J., & Jarosz, A. F. (2012b). How working memory capacity affects problem solving. In B. H. Ross (Ed.), *Psychology of learning and motivation* (Vol. 56, pp. 185–227). Burlington: Academic Press. doi:10.1016/B978-0-12-394393-4.00006-6

Zabelina, D. L., & Robinson, M. D. (2010). Creativity as flexible cognitive control. *Psychology of Aesthetics, Creativity, and the Arts*, 4(3), 136–143. doi:10.1037/a0017379

Chapter 5
Individual Creativity:
Predictors and Characteristics

ABSTRACT

It is well documented that creativity is possible for most people. Having the potential for creativity does not necessarily mean that all people communicate or utilize creative thinking. The issue is potential versus actualization and communication of creativity. How to identify factors that connect to creativity and determine if current or future employees are creative pose interesting issues. Connections between the psychological constructs of intelligence, personality, intrinsic motivation and creativity would seem logical venues of study to identify creative thinking. However, the research remains inconclusive as to why some people excel in creativity and others do not. Identifying creative employees is important for employers in the future workplace to intentionally provide model thinking and stronger team productivity.

INTRODUCTION: SQUARE WATERMELONS

There are many motivations for discovering creative solutions: some are fueled by the need to solve a creative problem in an academic setting, but many are from a very real need that arises in the real world. It is, in fact, quite common to encounter issues or challenges in the real world that cannot be solved with typical, linear solutions. One such example represents a very practical need that did not have an immediate, obvious solution. The problem is as follows: "Japanese grocery stores had a problem. They are much smaller than their

Individual Creativity

US counterparts and therefore don't have room to waste. Watermelons, big and round, wasted a lot of space" (Knox, 2015). Take a moment now and think about how you would solve this dilemma- what recommendations would you make to the businesses in Japan to make it possible for them to continue selling watermelons?

There are a number of ways to tackle this issue- some more creative and some less creative than others. Arguably, the most obvious solution would be to enlarge the stores in Japan to allow for more space to store watermelon. However, there are a number of reasons why this solution won't work- after all, square footage added to one space takes square footage away from another, equally important, space. Another obvious and easy solution would be to simply stop selling watermelon in Japan. It is evident that if there are no watermelons to sell, there does not need to be a place to display them, and therefore there would no longer be an issue. From a business perspective, however, neither of these solutions is ideal. Realistically, either of the above solutions would likely hurt your bottom-line, not to mention the industry of watermelon farming that would be lay to waste. What, then, should grocery retailers in Japan to do about this conundrum?

Many people would simply tell the grocery stores that watermelons grow round and there is nothing that can be done about it- the watermelon lovers in Japan would just be out of luck. Thankfully, a creative and innovative solution has been found. Japanese farmers invented the square watermelon, which, not only made it possible for the grocery stores to keep watermelon in stock, but also made shipping more efficient and cost effective (Knox, 2015). It turns out the solution is actually quite simple- if you put watermelon in a square box while they are still growing they will grow to fit the box and the result is a space-saving, stackable, square shaped watermelon (Knox, 2015).

What can we take from the square watermelon example? According to Knox (2015) there are at least five lessons we should take away from the story:

1. **Don't Assume:** One of the biggest hurdles that had to be overcome to solve the watermelon dilemma was assumption- and we all know what happens when we assume things. One of the foundations of creative problem solving lies in breaking assumptions about what is or what can be.
2. **Question Habits:** The antithesis of creativity is to do things like they've always been done without questioning why they are done that way or

whether or not the way they are done could be improved. Much like the story of the woman who always cut her pot roast in half to cook it because that's the way her mother did it (the pot roast principle), forcing yourself to question *why* you do things the way you do can be the initiating force for change.
3. **Look For a Better Way:** Finding a better, more innovative way to do things is contingent upon searching for it. Often times a "better way" is not just going to reveal itself to you- to initiate the process one must make a habit of asking if there is a better way and what that better way may look like.
4. **Impossibilities Often Aren't:** Many possible things seem impossible at first. Rather than asking yourself- is this possible, switch to *how* is this possible? Such a simple distinction can make an immeasurable difference in the likelihood of success on challenging endeavors.
5. **Be Creative:** Above and beyond questioning the status quo and noticing that there needs to be a better way to do something- it is vital to think outside the box to come up with a non-linear, non-obvious solution to a seemingly impossible problem. (Knox, 2015)

An additional bonus to inventing the square watermelon- because consumers love that the watermelon take up less space, farmers can charge a premium for their unique fruit (or vegetable depending on your perspective) (Knox, 2015).

This story is a particularly powerful example of the creative potential found in all people, not just the elite CEOs or Einsteins of the world. A theme that has been peppered throughout the chapters in this book is that everyone has the potential to be creative. Research from multiple sources supports the idea that creativity is possible for all people. In chapter two there was discussion concerning the many myths surrounding creative thinking and people which could influence the perceptions of value and influence the acceptance of fit in work environments. In chapter three there was information about how school environments can influence the development of creative thinking through socialization during crucial years of development. The fourth chapter makes the argument that creativity is the outcome of everyday processes that take place in our prefrontal cortex. In fact, the final point in the chapter is that "we are all equipped with a brain that is complex enough for us to think creatively." It is important to note, however, that having the potential to be engaged in creative thought does not automatically mean that one will do so. After all, you can lead a person to creativity, but you can't make them think.

Individual Creativity

How, then, can we begin to unravel what conditions or factors increase the likelihood that a person will generate in creative processes? If we all have the potential to be creative, but often fail to live up to that potential, what other factors are at play that are related to the likelihood we will be more creative? In this chapter the authors explore these questions and provide a list of possible characteristics for use to identify creativity in adults.

Objectives

The purpose of this chapter is to identify connections between the psychological constructs of intelligence, personality, intrinsic motivation, and to provide readers with some identifying behaviors of creative people. What is it about certain individuals that makes it more or less likely for them to engage in creative thinking? First, the authors will consider predictors of creativity and newer research that raises questions about thinking about creativity. Next, ways to identify creativity will be provided. After reading this chapter the reader should have better understanding of factors that influence individual creative thinking and some of the possible connections to other constructs.

BACKGROUND: CREATIVE PROFILES

Quality is more important than quantity. One home run is much better than two doubles. - Steve Jobs (1995)

Many researchers have attempted to determine what it is that makes some more creative than others, even though we all have the potential to be creative. Lee and Min (2016), for example, constructed creative profiles of 236 adults who were professionals in domains such as business, public service, law, medicine, research, education, and journalism. Creativity was measured based on the five subscales of the Torrance Tests of Creative Thinking (TTCT) (Torrance, 1966): fluency, originality, elaboration, abstractness of titles and resistance to premature closure. Overall, results indicated that there were distinctive profiles of creative characteristics based on professional domain. Specifically, the business professionals who participated in the study showed strength in the creativity dimension of fluency (number of ideas generated for questions) and weakness in the creativity dimension of resistance to premature closure (a measure of openness).

In other words, business professionals scored high in their ability to generate ideas, but low in their degree of openness or keeping an open mind. This may be due, at least in part, to the nature of the expectations of the business profession or it could be that individuals with these creative characteristics are drawn to certain careers. Yet another possibility is that the working environment surrounding this group of workers supports flexibility and ingenuity. Whatever the influences, thinking about what conditions move people to reach and communicate their creative potential is important. In the following section we will consider various predictors of creativity and the individual differences that are related to creative thinking processes.

PREDICTORS OF CREATIVITY

Researchers have been working to identify individual differences related to creativity for decades. Hayes (1989), for example, highlighted a number of individual differences related to creativity: IQ, devotion to work, independence, the drive for originality, and flexibility. More recent work has focused primarily on IQ or intelligence, personality factors, and intrinsic motivation (Tai & Mai, 2016; Weisberg, 2010). The next sections of this chapter will focus exclusively on these individual difference variables and the research that supports their relationships to creativity.

Intelligence and Creativity

There is ample evidence to support that intelligence is related to creativity (Batey, Furnham & Safiullina, 2010; Kim, 2005; Silvia, 2008; Simonton, 2000; Sternberg & O'Hara, 1999). The strength and nature of that relationship, however, is less clear. It is common for researchers to find a modest relationship between the two (Batey & Furnham, 2006; Kim 2005), but other researchers insist the relationship between the two is stronger and more stable than those results suggest. A meta-analysis was conducted on nearly 100 studies dating back to 1961 that investigated the relationship between intelligence and creativity (Kim, 2005). Results indicated a stable, but moderate relationship between the intelligence and creativity. Although the relationship was positive (indicating that increased intelligence was coupled with increased creativity), the authors argue that the strength of the relationship was so low ($r = 0.174$) that interpretations should be made cautiously (Kim, 2005).

Other researchers emphasize that the role of intelligence in creative thinking should not be over-looked (Silvia, 2008). Silvia (2008) conducted a latent variable model analysis and found a better supported relationship between general intelligence and creativity such that general intelligence predicted creativity scores as measured by unusual uses tasks. Similarly, Batey, Furnham & Safiullina (2010) found fluid intelligence to be a strong and consistent predictor of creativity (measured by divergent thinking tasks). What could be the explanation for such seemingly contradictory findings?

Historically, creativity researchers settled on the "threshold hypothesis" which suggested that there is a positive relationship between creativity and intelligence up to a certain level of intelligence (IQ of 120) and beyond that there was no relationship between the two (Guilford, 1967). This would suggest that as IQ increases so does creativity, but only up to a certain point- once a person surpasses the "magical" IQ cut off of 120 there is little to no relationship between creativity and intelligence. This would imply that intelligence is a necessary, but not sufficient condition for creativity. In fact, Karwowski et al., 2016 utilized a necessary condition analysis and found support for this notion. In other words, these findings support that a certain level of intelligence is necessary to engage in creative thought, but having that level of intelligence does not guarantee that one will be highly creative.

Although researchers have yet to reach a unanimous explanation for why there is a relationship between intelligence and creativity, there are a number of potential explanations. Some consider creativity to be sub-set of intelligence or vice versa while others emphasize that the two are unique and distinct constructs (Jauk, Benedek, Dunst & Neubauer, 2013; Sternberg & O'Hara, 1999). This is particularly difficult to determine definitively, but one thing is certain- there is a great deal of overlap in the types of processing that are indicative of both intelligence and creativity (Kaufman & Plucker, 2011). It is likely that the pre frontal cortex is associated with the types of processing indicative of both (Kane & Engle, 2002).

Personality and Creativity

There are a number of personality factors that have been shown to be associated with individual creativity. For example, Tai and Mai (2016) demonstrated a link between employee's proactive personality (an individual's disposition to take initiatives, seek out opportunities, and drive change) and organizational innovative capability through employee creativity. Two other personality factors, in particular, have been consistently associated with creativity- openness to experience and extroversion (Batey, Chamorro-Premuzic, & Furnham, 2010; Carson, Peterson & Higgins, 2005; Da Costa, Páez, Sánchez, Garaigordobil, & Gondim, 2015; Hirsh & Peterson, 2008; Kaufman et al., 2016; Madrid & Patterson, 2016; Silvia, 2008). Various analyses show that openness is has a closer relationship with creativity than does extroversion (or intelligence)- and often when both are put into predictive models openness remains and extroversion becomes non-significant (King, Walker, & Broyles, 1996 as cited in Hirsh, 2015; Silvia, 2008). Openness is one of the Big Five personality categories- along with conscientiousness, extraversion, agreeableness, and neuroticism (Costa & McCrae, 2008; Goldberg, 1993; McCrae & John, 1992). Scores on the Big Five personality dimensions are typically assessed through self-report on some version of the Big Five questionnaire. For example, one may be asked to what degree they agree with the following statements: "I am curious about many different things" or "I have a vivid imagination." People who score low on the openness personality dimension tend to have a narrow range of interests and often prefer engaging in more familiar than novel experiences. Conversely, people who score high on the openness personality dimension are notoriously curious, tend to enjoy learning about and experiencing new things, and have a wide variety of interests. This construct is supported by Robert Epstein's (1991; 1996; 1999) recommendations for creativity measurement which he categorizes as broadening or openness to learning new things and intellectual curiosity.

What could explain this relationship between openness and creativity? There is evidence to suggest that higher scores on the openness personality and reduced latent inhibition (Peterson & Carson, 2000; Peterson, Smith & Carson, 2002). You may recall from Chapter 4- latent inhibition (or inhibitory control) is one of the key mechanisms related to creativity. As stated in Chapter 4, latent inhibition "is the brain's capacity to screen out information deemed irrelevant- a way to focus attention on those aspects that are most relevant to the task at hand." It could be that there is a relationship between openness and creativity because they are both outcomes of the same cognitive mechanism- inhibitory control.

Intrinsic Motivation and Creativity

Motivation is an important aspect of virtually every thing we do in life. We all know how difficult it can be to force ourselves to engage in tasks that we find uninteresting or non-rewarding. It turns out there are a variety of types of motivations and reasons for which one might engage in a particular task. One of the most popular of these types of motivation is intrinsic motivation- "the degree to which people engage in an activity primarily because they find the activity itself to be interesting, enjoyable, and challenging" (Amabile & Pillemer, 2012 as cited in Liu, Jiang, Shalley, Keem & Zhou, 2016, pg. 237). There is evidence to support a relationship between intrinsic motivation and creativity (Amabile, 1996; Liu, et al., 2016; Mumford, 2003; Sternberg, 2006). This relationship suggests that intrinsic motivation is beneficial to creativity (Collins & Amabile, 1999). Further, creative individuals tend to be "energized by challenging tasks, a sign of high intrinsic motivation" (Collins & Amabile, 1999, pg. 300). Chapter six further explores more comprehensive effects of reward systems in relation to the workplace between intrinsic and extrinsic motivation.

CHANGING TECHNOLOGY FOR IDENTIFICATION OF CREATIVITY: ISSUES, PROBLEMS, AND CONTROVERSIES

The relationships among creativity and each of the individual differences discussed above most likely has their roots in neural activity in the prefrontal cortex (see Chapter 4 in this book for a more detailed argument). As the study of creativity has expanded to include brain neurology, however, some scientists question whether any standard definition, and the tests used to construct it, still make sense. This notion has the potential to make identification of creative elements in individuals particularly difficult. John Kounios (2010), a psychologist at Drexel University, argues that the standard has outlived its usefulness as creativity is a complex concept, not a single identifiable thing. Creativity is an important human characteristic. It is perhaps best thought of as a process, requiring a mixture of ingredients, including personality traits, abilities, and skills (Kounios, et al., 2006; Kounios, 2010). The brain appears to be an efficient superhighway that gets one from Point A to Point B when it comes to intelligence, but in the regions of the brain related to creativity, there appears to be lots of little side roads with interesting detours and meandering little byways. A traditional definition of creativity, the ability to combine novelty and usefulness in a particular social context, is changing as technology changes access to the working of the brain. While intelligence and skill are associated with the fast and efficient firing of neurons in the brain, subjects who tested high in creativity had thinner white matter and connecting axons that slow nerve traffic. Creativity corresponds with slower nerve traffic. Likewise, openness to experience (an individual difference associated with creativity) corresponds with slower nerve traffic. What this may mean to the research and applications of creativity is still unknown. As the field of brain neurology continues to explore creativity through technology, the concept of creativity may move into totally new approaches to identification, development, and sustainability across age groups.

While intelligence, personality and intrinsic motivation seem to relate to creativity, it remains inconclusive how or why some individuals appear more creative or perhaps comfortable communicating creative thinking. As more precise forms of technological evolve the brain paths may hold the answers to what triggers individual creativity.

The question remains as how do managers, human resources and others identify creative employees? What are some identifying behaviors of creative thinking?

SOLUTIONS AND RECOMMENDATIONS: WAYS TO MEASURE CREATIVITY

There are several reasons employers might want to identify creativity in individual employees when hiring or already employed. Creative people actively seek new solutions to problems, are comfortable with ambiguity, curious, willing to communicate creative thinking, serve as models for professional development of other workers, and look beyond information to find connections. Consequently, identifying creative applicants or existing employees can help improve the intentional working climate in any profession.

Informal Observations

Leslee Owens Wilson (n.d.) on her professional web page adapted a list of creative characteristics from from Renzulli and Hartman's (1971) inventory to identify creative behaviors. She presents some characteristics one can seek in future employees. Wilson claims that no one trait is a determining variable for creative thinking but that highly creative people have clusters of these

Individual Creativity

characteristics. This may explain why the research on single constructs and creativity are so inconsistent.

One way to determine potential for creative employees is through observations during personal and professional interactions, discussions and informal interviews using the following clusters.

Highly creative individuals may:

1. Display a great deal of curiosity about many things; are constantly asking questions about anything and everything; may have broad interests in many unrelated areas. May devise collections based on unusual things and interests.
2. Generate a large number of ideas or solutions to problems and questions; often offer unusual ("way out"), unique, clever responses.
3. Are often uninhibited in expressions of opinion; are sometimes radical and spirited in disagreement; are unusually tenacious or persistent — fixating on an idea or project.
4. Are willing to take risks, are often people who are described as a "high risk taker, or adventurous, or speculative."
5. Exhibit a good deal of intellectual playfulness; may frequently be caught fantasizing, daydreaming or imagining. Often wonder out loud and might be heard saying, "I wonder what would happen if . . ."; or "What if we change. . . ." Can manipulate ideas by easily changing, elaborating, adapting, improving, or modifying the original idea or the ideas of others." Are often concerned with improving the conceptual frameworks of institutions, objects, and systems.
6. Have keen senses of humor and see comicality in situations that may not appear to be humorous to others. Sometimes what they find funny, comic, or amusing may appear bizarre, inappropriate, or irreverent to others.
7. Are unusually aware of his or her impulses and are often more open to the irrational within him or herself. May freely display opposite gender characteristics— may be androgynous (freer expression of feminine interests in boys, or as males they are considered ultra sensitive, or greater than usual amount of independence, assertiveness, or aggressiveness for females).
8. Exhibit heightened emotional sensitivity. May be very sensitive to beauty, and visibly moved by aesthetic experiences.
9. Are frequently perceived as nonconforming; can often accept the disorder of chaotic environments or situations; are frequently not interested in

details, are described as individualistic; or do not fear being classified as "different."
10. Criticize constructively, and are unwilling to accept authoritarian pronouncements without overly critical self-examination (Owens, n.d.).

During the interviewing and hiring process, focusing on these characteristics will allow candidates who are able to demonstrate their creativity and innovative capabilities and "rise above the pack" (Grefe, 2011). With already hired employees, identification of these individuals who demonstrate strong creative capabilities can provide information for team grouping, initiative leaders, or provide a model of thinking to other employees. This allows for a great deal of promise for collaborative work fostering creative and innovative processes. However the information is used, identification of creative characteristics in individuals is needed to ensure that businesses remain on the forefront of innovation in an ever-changing world.

Formal Inventories

While there seems to be no one right, foolproof, approach to identifying creativity in individual employees, it is increasingly important to look for characteristics associated with this attribute. There are multiple creativity inventories that have been developed to provide creativity ratings of individuals-many of which have been developed for gifted and talented education programs. Although many are focused on detecting creative characteristics in children or young adults, some are appropriate for use with all ages. For example, two well-known and validated instruments are rooted in Epstein's work on creativity: the Epstein Creativity Competencies Inventory (ECCI-i)(Epstein, Schmidt, & Warfel, 2008), and Torrance's (1966; 1972) renowned Test of Creative Thinking (TCTT). Many of the creativity instruments, including the ECCI-i and the TTCT, are available online (Epstein: http://drrobertepstein.com/index.php/tests and Torrance: http://www.ststesting.com/ngifted.html). A number of other validated instruments have been developed to measure creativity and creative potential in individuals, results of which, can and perhaps should be used to consider the creative potential of potential employees.

FUTURE RESEARCH DIRECTIONS

A point made consistently across the chapters in this book is that there is no isolated "creative gene" that accounts for all creative potential in the individual. Rather, a more integrated view of the predictors of creativity is needed to better, and more reliably, identify persons with strong creative potential. Further, an integrated view of creative potential is needed to determine factors of creativity that can (and should) be nurtured in the individual. Although all of us have the potential to be highly creative, most of us fail to realize that full potential. A vertical alignment of research across domains to span children through adulthood to determine environmental, neurological connections and sustainability of creative processing is needed to better understand a more full model of the creative process and the factors associated with it. That is not to suggest that there is a perfect "recipe" for creativity, but rather, that consideration of a more integrated model of creative processing has the potential to lead to a more accurate and reliable way to better nurture creative processes in individuals.

Because individuals have the potential to enhance various elements of their creative performance a fruitful direction for future research would be to determine the ways individuals con progress on each of the elements associated with creativity. A set of creativity progressions needs to be identified to determine a more seamless identification of elements and strategies to foster creative thought. Creativity progressions should be constructed not only for each of the elements that predict creative thought, but also for the construct of creativity as a whole.

CONCLUSION

Creativity is complex. Defining creativity is more complex. Identifying creativity is even more complex. However, ways to identify those individuals with great creative potential and identify aspects of creativity that should be fostered in individuals remains a strong desire of those who wish to be a part of innovative, cutting edge businesses. This creates a paradox where the thing we want (maximized creative potential) is the very thing that is so elusive and difficult to define. What, then, should employers do?

Fortunately, there are some behaviors that are indicative of creative thought in individuals. Unfortunately, we are still awaiting a more comprehensive model of creativity that takes all of these behaviors, neurological correlates, and environmental factors into account. As a starting point, awareness of these behaviors, correlates and environmental factors may help employers identify creative people in their workplaces and during initial hiring interviews. Further, it may help businesses in making decisions about how to best optimize creativity and innovation with their current workforce. Identification of creative profiles for individuals can also help foster optimal creativity at the team level. Workers with profiles suggesting weakness in particular areas of creativity can be paired with individuals who demonstrate the opposite strength and vice versa. Creative powerhouse teams could be more accurately developed to maximize creative potential and thrust innovation forward in the business world.

REFERENCES

Amabile, T. M. (1996). *Creativity in context: Update to the social psychology of creativity*. Boulder, CO: Westview.

Amabile, T. M., & Pillemer, J. (2012). Perspectives on the social psychology of creativity. *The Journal of Creative Behavior, 46*(1), 3–15. doi:10.1002/jocb.001

Batey, M., Chamorro-Premuzic, T., & Furnham, A. (2010). Individual differences in ideational behavior: Can the big five and psychometric intelligence predict creativity scores? *Creativity Research Journal, 22*(1), 90–97. doi:10.1080/10400410903579627

Batey, M., & Furnham, A. (2006). Creativity, intelligence, and personality: A critical review of the scattered literature. *Genetic, Social, and General Psychology Monographs, 132*(4), 355–429. doi:10.3200/MONO.132.4.355-430 PMID:18341234

Batey, M., Furnham, A., & Safiullina, X. (2010). Intelligence, general knowledge and personality as predictors of creativity. *Learning and Individual Differences, 20*(5), 532–535. doi:10.1016/j.lindif.2010.04.008

Carson, S. H., Peterson, J. B., & Higgins, D. M. (2005). Reliability, validity, and factor structure of the creative achievement questionnaire. *Creativity Research Journal, 17*(1), 37–50. doi:10.1207/s15326934crj1701_4

Collins, M. A., & Amabile, T. M. (1999). Motivation and creativity. In R. J. Sternberg (Ed.) Handbook of Creativity (pp. 297-312). New York, NY: Cambridge.

Costa, P. T., & McCrae, R. R. (2008). The revised neo personality inventory (neo-pi-r). The SAGE handbook of personality theory and assessment, 2, 179-198.

Da Costa, S., Páez, D., Sánchez, F., Garaigordobil, M., & Gondim, S. (2015). Personal factors of creativity: A second order meta-analysis. *Revista de Psicología del Trabajo y de las Organizaciones*, *31*(3), 165–173. doi:10.1016/j.rpto.2015.06.002

Epstein, R. (1991). Skinner, Creativity, and the Problem of Spontaneous Behavior. *Psychological Science*, 6(6), 362–370. doi:10.1111/j.1467-9280.1991.tb00168.x

Epstein, R. (1996). *Cognition, Creativity, and Behavior: Selected Essays.* Westport, CT: Praeger.

Epstein, R. (1999). Generativity Theory. In M. A. Runco & S. Pritzker (Eds.), Encyclopedia of Creativity (pp. 759–766). Academic Press.

Epstein, R., Schmidt, S. M., & Warfel, R. (2008). Measuring and Training Creativity Competencies: Validation of a New Test. *Creativity Research Journal*, *20*(1), 7–12. doi:10.1080/10400410701839876

Goldberg, L. R. (1993). The structure of phenotypic personality traits. *The American Psychologist*, *48*(1), 26–34. doi:10.1037/0003-066X.48.1.26 PMID:8427480

Grefe, R. (2011). *What are employers looking for in a creative professional?* The Professional Association for Design. Retrieved from http://www.aiga.org/what-are-employers-looking-for-in-a-creative-professional

Guilford, J. P. (1967). *The nature of human intelligence.* New York: McGraw-Hill.

Hayes, J. R. (1989). Cognitive processes in creativity. In Handbook of creativity (pp. 135-145). Springer US. doi:10.1007/978-1-4757-5356-1_7

Hirsh, J. B. (2015). Personality and creativity. International Encyclopedia of the Social and Behavioral Sciences, 17, 770-773.

Hirsh, J. B., & Peterson, J. B. (2008). Predicting creativity and academic success with a fake-proof measure of the Big Five. *Journal of Research in Personality, 42*(5), 1323–1333. doi:10.1016/j.jrp.2008.04.006

Jauk, E., Benedek, M., Dunst, B., & Neubauer, A. C. (2013). The relationship between intelligence and creativity: New support for the threshold hypothesis by means of empirical breakpoint detection. *Intelligence, 41*(4), 212–221. doi:10.1016/j.intell.2013.03.003 PMID:23825884

Jobs, S. (1995). *Steve Jobs interview from Triumph of the nerds.* PBS. Retrieved from http://www.pbs.org/nerds/

Kane, M. J., & Engle, R. W. (2002). The role of prefrontal cortex in working-memory capacity, executive attention, and general fluid intelligence: An individual-differences perspective. *Psychonomic Bulletin & Review, 9*(4), 637–671. doi:10.3758/BF03196323 PMID:12613671

Karwowski, M., Dul, J., Gralewski, J., Jauk, E., Jankowska, D. M., Gajda, A., & Benedek, M. et al. (2016). Is creativity without intelligence possible? A necessary condition analysis. *Intelligence, 57*, 105–117. doi:10.1016/j.intell.2016.04.006

Kaufman, J. C., & Plucker, J. A. (2011). Intelligence and creativity. In R. J. Sternberg & S. B. Kaufman (Eds.), The handbook of intelligence (pp. 771-783). Cambridge, UK: Cambridge University. doi:10.1017/CBO9780511977244.039

Kaufman, S. B., Quilty, L. C., Grazioplene, R. G., Hirsh, J. B., Gray, J. R., Peterson, J. B., & DeYoung, C. G. (2016). Openness to experience and intellect differentially predict creative achievement in the arts and sciences. *Journal of Personality, 84*(2), 248–258. doi:10.1111/jopy.12156 PMID:25487993

Kim, K. H. (2005). Can only intelligent people be creative? A meta-analysis. *Journal of Secondary Gifted Education, 16*(2-3), 57–66. doi:10.4219/jsge-2005-473

King, L. A., Walker, L. M., & Broyles, S. J. (1996). Creativity and the five-factor model. *Journal of Research in Personality, 30*(2), 189–203. doi:10.1006/jrpe.1996.0013

Knox, D. (2015, October 19). Lessons of the square watermelon [Blog post]. Retrieved from https://hardknoxlife.com/lessons-of-the-square-watermelon-b0fe06a6c901

Kounios, J. (2010, May 8). Charting creativity: Signposts of a hazy territory. *New York Times*, p. C1.

Kounios, J., Frymiare, J. L., Bowden, E. M., Fleck, J. I., Subramaniam, K., Parrish, T. B., & Jung-Beeman, M. J. (2006). The prepared mind: Neural activity prior to problem presentation predicts subsequent solution by sudden insight. *Psychological Science*, *17*(10), 882–890. doi:10.1111/j.1467-9280.2006.01798.x PMID:17100789

Lee, S. Y., & Min, J. (2016). The profiles of creative potential and personality characteristics of adult professionals. *Creativity Research Journal*, *28*(3), 298–309. doi:10.1080/10400419.2016.1195634

Liu, D., Jiang, K., Shalley, C. E., Keem, S., & Zhou, J. (2016). Motivational mechanisms of employee creativity: A meta-analytic examination and theoretical extension of the creativity literature. *Organizational Behavior and Human Decision Processes*, *137*, 236–263. doi:10.1016/j.obhdp.2016.08.001

Madrid, H. P., & Patterson, M. G. (2016). Creativity at work as a joint function between openness to experience, need for cognition and organizational fairness. *Learning and Individual Differences*, *51*, 409–416. doi:10.1016/j.lindif.2015.07.010

McCrae, R. R., & John, O. P. (1992). An introduction to the five-factor model and its applications. *Journal of Personality*, *60*(2), 175–215. doi:10.1111/j.1467-6494.1992.tb00970.x PMID:1635039

Mumford, M. D. (2003). Where have we been, where are we going? Taking stock in creativity research. *Creativity Research Journal*, *15*(2-3), 107–120. doi:10.1080/10400419.2003.9651403

Peterson, J. B., & Carson, S. (2000). Latent inhibition and openness to experience in a high-achieving student population. *Personality and Individual Differences*, *28*(2), 323–332. doi:10.1016/S0191-8869(99)00101-4

Peterson, J. B., Smith, K. W., & Carson, S. (2002). Openness and extraversion are associated with reduced latent inhibition: Replication and commentary. *Personality and Individual Differences*, *33*(7), 1137–1147. doi:10.1016/S0191-8869(02)00004-1

Renzulli, J., & Hartman, R. (1971). Scale for rating the behavioral characteristics of superior students. *Exceptional Children*, *38*(3), 243–248. doi:10.1177/001440297103800309

Silvia, P. J. (2008). Another look at creativity and intelligence: Exploring higher-order models and probable confounds. *Personality and Individual Differences, 44*(4), 1012–1021. doi:10.1016/j.paid.2007.10.027

Simonton, D. K. (2000). Creativity: Cognitive, personal, developmental, and social aspects. *The American Psychologist, 55*(1), 151–158. doi:10.1037/0003-066X.55.1.151 PMID:11392859

Sternberg, R. J. (2006). The nature of creativity. *Creativity Research Journal, 18*(1), 87–98. doi:10.1207/s15326934crj1801_10

Sternberg, R. J., & O'Hara, L. A. (1999). Creativity and intelligence. In R. J. Sternberg (Ed.), Handbook of Creativity (pp. 251-272). New York, NY: Cambridge.

Tai, H. T., & Mai, N. Q. (2016). Proactive personality, organizational context, employee creativity and innovative capability: Evidence from MNCs and domestic corporations. *The International Journal of Organizational Analysis, 24*(3), 370–389. doi:10.1108/IJOA-04-2015-0857

Torrance, E. P. (1966). Torrance Tests of Creative Thinking: Normstechnical Manual: Research Ed.: Verbal Tests, Forms A and B: Figural Tests, Forms A and B. Flere Materialer. Princeton, NJ: Personell Press.

Torrance, E. P. (1972). *Predictive validity of the Torrance tests of creative thinking. The Journal of Creative Behavior, 6(4), 236—262.* doi:10.1002/j.2162-6057.1972.tb00936.x

Weisberg, R. (2010). The study of creativity: From genius to cognitive science. *International Journal of Cultural Policy, 16*(3), 235–253. doi:10.1080/10286630903111639

Wilson, L. O. (n.d.) The second principle. *Characteristics of highly creative people.* Retrieved from http://thesecondprinciple.com/creativity/creativetraits/

Chapter 6
Creative Transformation:
Setting the Stage for Workplace Creativity and Innovation

ABSTRACT

Creative transformation is the term associated with the necessary change for the workplace to develop and support creative thinking, which leads to innovation. Managing the intricacies of any workplace is a delicate balance. The issue is keeping the workflow efficiently moving forward while simultaneously providing an environment that encourages creativity and innovation. Complacency and comfort with "tried and true" methods constitute a path of least resistance, which may partially explain why change in any environment is so difficult. Ultimately, it is time for a new era in the workplace- an era of creativity that will redefine how organizations function. Creativity is a bigger predictor of success in life and work than many other factors, even intelligence and can be learned and nurtured when supported in the workplace. Creativity is the new literacy and it is time for the workplace to reflect that.

INTRODUCTION: A TALE OF CORPORATE THINKING

Every day, a small Ant arrived at work early and starting work immediately, she produced a lot and she was happy. The boss, a lion, was surprised to see that the ant was working without supervision. He thought if the ant can produce so much without supervision, wouldn't she produce more if she had a supervisor!

So the lion recruited a cockroach who had extensive experience as a supervisor and who was famous for writing excellent reports. The cockroach's first decision was to set up a clocking in attendance system. He also needed a secretary to help him write and type his reports. He recruited a spider who managed the archives and monitored all phone calls.

The Lion was delighted with the cockroach's report and asked him to produce graphs to describe production rates and analyze trends so that he could use them for presentations at board meetings. So the cockroach had to buy a new computer and a laser printer and recruit a fly to manage the IT department. The Ant, who had been once so productive and relaxed, hated this new plethora of paperwork and meetings, which used up most of her time.

The lion came to the conclusion that it was high time to nominate a person in charge of the department where the ant worked. The position was given to the Cicada whose first decision was to buy a carpet and an ergonomic chair for his office. The new person in charge, the cicada, also needed a computer and a personal assistant, whom he had brought from his previous department to help him prepare a work and budget control strategic optimization plan.

The department where the ant works is now a sad place, where nobody laughs anymore and everybody has become upset. It was at that time the cicada convinced the boss, the Lion, to start a climatic study of the office environment. Having reviewed the charges of running the ant's department, the lion found out that the production was much less than before so he recruited the Owl, a prestigious and renowned consultant to carry out an audit and suggest solutions. The Owl spent 3 months in the department and came out with an enormous report, in several volumes, that concluded that "The Department is overstaffed."

Guess who the lion fired first?

The Ant, of course, "Because she showed lack of motivation and had a negative attitude." - (Noone, 2010).

Creative Transformation

The above fable portrays the traditional organizational structure found in many workplaces. Often larger organizations rely heavily on routines, procedures and processes which have delivered success in the past. While the traditional approaches to organizational structure may seem important, the bottom line is how the work environment influences the productivity of the actual worker. Many organizations claim they want a more creative and innovative workplace yet continue to provide a traditional working environment. In order to stimulate creativity, employers must first create a great work place environment where employees are encouraged to contribute. Attention must be paid to whether the employees like their workplace and how the environment supports creativity.

There are multiple perspectives on the creative environment, yet there is limited research available. This chapter addresses the workplace environment and components that influence creativity to foster innovation. According to Hoff (2014) traditional creativity models often address what is called the four P- components: the creative person(s), the creative process, the creative product and the creative place. The environment of the workplace, or the creative place, is vital for developing and supporting creative work. Workplace transformation results in increased employee engagement and ultimately, competitive advantage for the organization (Cher, 2015). The authors believe that there are several opportunities for creative workplace transformation and that reward systems must be varied to support the workers in any organization for innovation to occur. This chapter will focus on the creative support systems through workplace transformation.

Objectives

The purpose of this chapter is to provide an overview of how different work environments can create a creative workplace transformational setting to allow workers to ideate and move towards innovation. After reading this chapter, one should gain an understanding of different components relating to transformational change as well as reflect on belief systems that may influence environmental settings and actions for change. The new generation of workers has different expectations of the workplace and support systems, which need to be addressed to provide environments to support optimal creativity in the maximum number of individuals.

BACKGROUND: ORGANIZATIONAL STRUCTURES, PRACTICES, AND POLICIES

Throughout my years in business, I discovered something. I would always ask why you do things. The answers that I would invariably get are: "Oh that's just the way things are done around here. Nobody knows why they do what they do." Nobody thinks very deeply about things in business. - Steve Jobs (n.d.)

Managing any workplace is a delicate balance between keeping the workflow moving forward while simultaneously providing an environment that encourages creativity and innovation. Creativity involves questioning prevailing norms which can be problematic if the organization prefers the status quo (Rasulzada, 2014). Sticking to past approaches can manifest itself into inflexibility, rigidity and a fear of the unknown, and lead to avoidance of creativity. In essense, what worked well for 30 years isn't necessarily working well today or will work well tomorrow. The entire organization needs to support learning, creative thinking and respect for all contributions of multilevel workers. And for learning to happen, that means admitting failure, identifying lessons learned, and most important, actually applying lessons learned (Gendron, 2017). This idea is very different from a workplace where failure is punished, rather than embraced as a step closer toward success as each attempt is analyzed and revised. Employees must have the freedom to fail, reflect and revise without repercussions.

People may be unaware of the influence of environmental norms on behavior and creative thinking. Work and social expectations are usually those accepted by the largest percentage of a culture. These are evident in any workplace; the system of acceptable dress and behavior is one prong to this. However, another is the comfort zone for different ideas and ways of thinking from the average or norm. Complacency and comfort with "tried and true" methods are a path of least resistance which may explain why environmental change is so difficult.

A study by Adobe and Forrester Consulting found that 82 percent of companies believe there is a strong connection between creativity and business results. In fact, companies that actively foster creative thinking outperform their rivals in revenue growth, market share and competitive leadership (Fallon, 2016). The environment of the workplace is vital for developing and supporting creative work. All organizations have creative people and they need to be encouraged if maximum success is to be achieved.

Because creativity can evoke different kinds of emotions across all levels of the working environment, it is important to be aware of how one perceives creative thinking. Is it a threat to perceived security? Does it involve chaos in the workplace? Is it embraced and supported? Creative problem-solving works best when harnessed with highly focused and disciplined thought. The trick is being rigorous, but not rigid, in your work.

CREATIVE TRANSFORMATION: REINVENTING THE WORKING ENVIRONMENT

Creating environments that are conducive for creative professionals is of interest to several disciplines (Hoff, 2014) and has become a global priority in this age designated as the knowledge society (Andersson & Stromquist, 1988; Hansen, 2008; Niedomysl, 2010) or the creative age (Florida, 2004/2012). The balance between rigorous but not rigid is a challenge for the creative transformation. Creativity needs structure to flourish but not so much structure that it is crushed (Fallon, 2014). Creativity combines two modes of thinking, divergent and convergent, for creative breakthrough. Divergent thinking generates creative ideas by exploring multiple solutions. Convergent focuses on identifying a solution based on the available data. Both are necessary for innovation.

Developing environments to support creativity that lead to innovation seem to include complex relationships among multiple variables. Hoff (2014) refers to these as cultural and psychosocial environmental factors that, along with the physical environment, impact creativity. Cultural and psychosocial are factors that could influence individuals through psychological and/or social mechanisms. However, the cultural aspect must also be considered as values and traditions are evident in the workplace dependent on the country or region.

Is this change easy? No- change is never easy, but by reinventing the corporate culture and the office environment to place more emphasis on creativity, organizations are reaping the benefits and becoming leaders in their respective industries (Genever, 2016). Not only does creative thinking produce winning sales and marketing campaigns that increase brand appeal to the end user, but [it] can also help foster a unique company culture that ultimately reflects and encourages creativity within each department (Taylor, 2016).

Geographic Transformation

Some urban areas are more conducive for creativity than others. According to results of a survey released by Adobe Systems Incorporated (2016) Tokyo was identified as the top creative city in the world. New York was second, followed by Paris, London, Las Angeles, San Francisco and Berlin. Japan was rated the most creative country worldwide by the survey's respondents, ahead of the United States and France. Andersson & Stormquist (1988) attribute this phenomenon to the advantages of a cosmopolitan area, creativity, culture, communication and competence. It is no accident, then, that creative businesses still choose to be in high density, mixed-use neighborhoods in big cities. However, an urban area alone is not enough to ensure high levels of creativity. These environments offer the best prospects for forming the relationships necessary for competing in the modern creative economy (Spenser, 2015). People who are high in openness-to-experience are also adventurous, likely to generate new views or perspectives on old approaches, and are comfortable with change. Ultimately, surrounding, or exposure to novel and ambiguous stimuli is important for creative environments.

Does this mean company's need to relocate? Of course not. Organizations that have transformed their workplace find employees are more productive and happier; it's easier to hire the best, most qualified candidates for your job openings because location no longer dictates success; and office space utilization will increase by only accommodating those who come into the office on a given day. The days of bosses expecting to see workers in by 9am, diligently typing away till late, are gone. In an interview with Maratin Duursma he argues that the twin trends of remote working and Bring Your Own Device (BYOD) is destined to change this equation for good (Cher, 2015).

One example is the Google international office in Tel Aviv (See Figure 1 for image), which transforms the workplace into a comfortable setting for conversation and incorporates unique aspects of the environment to provide interesting work sites (including an indoor orange grove). The space gives employees the right tools for work, but also those to motivate and foster inspiration and creativity. There are three restaurants located in the eight-floor office space. Seven floors are designed to create communication landscapes, comfortable places for workers to communicate and collaborate. There is traditional desk space combined with open design to serve all working styles One floor is an innovative Google "Campus" opened by the Israeli Prime Minister where entrepreneurs and developers can meet and develop start-up companies, powered by Google for entrepreneurs.

Figure 1. Tel Aviv Google office design gives workers an interesting workspace
(https://officesnapshots.com/2013/01/31/google-tel-aviv-office-design/)

Let's face it- it is not always feasible to incorporate an orange grove into your office, but it is possible to set up exposure to new ideas in any workplace. Florida and Knudson (2004), for example, found that the new class of creative workers does not move to where the jobs are but settle in places they find interesting to live in or companies that provide interesting work environments. Ultimately, the goal is to create a work environment that is stimulating and interesting to workers and that is flexible enough to accommodate the various needs of the local workforce.

Cultural Transformation

Culture refers to the unique workplace environment that should be culturally rich and diverse. Steve Jobs was considered a master at bringing people together with different backgrounds and arranging productive teams. He brought people with different careers, diverse backgrounds, and interests together and gave them freedom and time to communicate through their interactions. Jobs emphasized the key to "thinking differently" is to perceive things differently; in order to perceive things differently, a leader must be exposed to divergent ideas, places and people. This will force your brain to make connections it otherwise might miss (Jobs, 1982). The idea of cultural diversity is further supported in an interview with Mike Mansbach, president of BlueJeans Network. Mansbach, shared that the more diverse a group's knowledge and beliefs are, the more diverse ideas and creative solutions will arise Fallon (2014). BlueJeans encourages a creative environment by using video technology for brainstorm sessions. This brings diversity to the workplace and allows businesses to easily connect people from different geographic locations, experience levels and specialties around the country to offer unique perspectives to problems. Regular brainstorming sessions with diverse groups of employees can also instill a sense of appreciation for unconventional thinking a key component to the transformational workplace.

Florida's (2012) conceptualization of the creative diversity climate consists of three words: tolerance, technology and talent. Culture falls under tolerance. He includes a mix of worker characteristics that include foreign born, bohemian and openness towards sexual diversity. However, diversity comes in many other forms as well. There is experience, age, gender, personality, job levels and ethnicity. The important point about this is the manager and workplace has no room for personal bias if creativity is to be nurtured. Teams need to include a mix of diverse workers to allow different worldviews to develop new ideas, refine old ideas and create new solutions to problems. One should also encourage diversity within these teams. For example, if you are making a team of people to work on a project, make sure they come from all different backgrounds including ethnicity, experience, seniority, and personality types. Creativity happens best at the intersection of disciplines. Most breakthrough discoveries occur when two or more disciplines collide (Taylor, 2016). Homogeneous (all members of a team with similar backgrounds) groups rarely bring innovations as they all share a common cultural background with accepted norms and a set of beliefs. Think of this as a steady diet of one food with no seasoning or spice variation, which could never produce new or exciting tastes. Variety, diversity and change bring new ideas and approaches to innovation.

Diverse teams are important to creative thinking; however, another major component is respecting diversity. All members of the team need to be valued. While this sounds simple, it may be overlooked. In fact, traditional homogeneous groups often take control of group work, isolating members who are different from the accepted norm. Steve Jobs (1982) believes that creative thinkers form a subculture within cultures. When he would put diverse people in a room he observed that creative thinkers would be drawn to each other across cultural groups. While this may be accurate, one must always remember that culture is emotion laden and belief systems are deeply ingrained in individuals. Tolerance is the start but moving towards acceptance is the next stage of respect.

Psychosocial Transformation

The term psychosocial relates to the combination of psychological and social behavior. Twenty years ago, this topic would have not been considered of importance in the workplace. Today, the relationship between emotional wellbeing and the environment has become a consideration in both schools and work. Factors such as stress, hostility and job control are connected to physical health. Psychosocial transformation underscores the close connection between psychological aspects of one's experiences and the social experience, which includes relationships, the working environment and culture. As the world has changed so has the need to consider the emotional and social interactions of employees in work environments.

Social Transformation

Social relationships are also an important influence in the creative workplace development and communication is a key aspect of fostering such relationships (Tai & Mai, 2016). In fact, communication and a positive atmosphere have been shown to have significant impacts on both individual and organizational creativity and innovation (Tai & Mai, 2016). We cannot escape that innovation, more and more, is a social activity. It occurs at the edges between teams, when people collide in unexpected places, to spark new ideas (Cher, 2015). Innovative work spaces often combine open spaces, comfortable seating areas, community work areas with fun activity centers to create an atmosphere in which coworkers can collaborate, throw ideas around, chat, and even take a break and bond in a social setting.

The new generation of workers is well accustomed with frequent social communication and spends a lot of time using electronic devices to connect over various social media platforms. It is a part of the current and future culture and finding ways to incorporate this into the workplace is important to social transformation. University faculty, for example, have learned that a "no electronic device policy" in the classroom can lead to unrealistic expectations of this new generation. Strict rules against these devices, rather than preventing their use during work or school, often have the opposite effect on younger workers and result in a mission to get on the devices without getting caught. Teachers, managers, and employers are fighting a losing battle to rid their environments of electronic devices. But is it a battle worth fighting? After all, digital platforms offer the potential to enhance worker productivity by fostering connections with colleagues and resources around the globe (Olmstead, Lampe. & Ellison. 2016).

One very real concern, particularly among management, is that employees are using these tools for non-work purposes while on the job or posting in public venues that might reflect poorly on their organization. In 2014, the PEW Research Center discovered that today's workforce use social platforms for a wide variety of purposes on the job. The survey asked Americans who are employed full- or part-time about eight different ways they might use social media while on the job and found that:

- 34% use social media while at work to take a mental break from their job.
- 27% to connect with friends and family while at work.
- 24% to make or support professional connections.
- 20% to get information that helps them solve problems at work.
- 17% to build or strengthen personal relationships with coworkers.
- 17% to learn about someone they work with.
- 12% to ask work-related questions of people *outside* their organization.
- 12% to ask such questions of people *inside* their organization.

Workers whose companies have policies regulating social media use at work are less likely to use social media in certain ways:

- 30% of workers whose companies have an at-work social media policy say they use social media while on the job to take a break from work, compared with 40% of workers whose employers do not have such policies.
- 20% of workers whose employers have at-work social media policies say they use social media to stay connected to family and friends while on the job, compared with 35% of workers whose social media use is not regulated at work.
- Only 16% of workers whose companies regulate social media at work say they use social media while working to get information that's helpful to their job, compared with 25% of those whose workplaces have no such regulations.

On the other hand, workers are equally likely to say they use social media for a range of purposes regardless of their workplace policy, including:

- Making or supporting professional contacts that help them do their job.
- Learning more about someone they work with.
- Building or strengthening personal relationships with coworkers.
- Asking work-related questions of people *outside* their organization.
- Asking work-related questions of people *inside* their organization. (PEW Research Center, 2014)

Realistically, even when restrictions are required, workers still use social media at work. Rather than continuing to fight a losing battle with social media the workplace needs to find productive uses that can support employees' growing use of these devices. The use of time on task is considered one of the main issues with social media use in the workplace. At one time employees took cigarette or coffee breaks during the day to clear their thinking- the new generation takes social media breaks. Some suggestions for use of social media are as follows:

- Use Facebook or Instagram as the office newsletter.
- Start chat rooms with identified issues or problems for solving related to the worksite.
- Set up a pair and share site where small working groups can post new ideas for discussion.
- Encourage communicating with other professionals and have a share out time to discuss new ideas or adaptations.
- Make a 10% rule, where employees are allowed to spend 10% of their day off work tasks.
- Allow social media breaks during the day for personal communication.

While the social media debate continues, use of these social systems continues to increase. This trend is not going away so the smart manager will use it to their advantage and find ways to use social media in the workplace.

Emotional Transformation

The workplace has become an important social support environment in the creativity age. This has brought attention to the emotional expectations of the new breed of workers. The old view of a manager's role did not consider emotional support as part of the job description. The new workforce perceives that managers are paid to provide emotional support (Chiswick Consulting, 2015). This is quite a large change in expectations and one that demands new approaches to interactions across all levels of the work environment. Sometimes something as simple as just listening to concerns helps provide support. Other times a more active planning approach is needed.

Another aspect of psychosocial transformation deals with the emotional environment by setting a stage for acceptance of ideas in a risk-free environment. Alex Osborn, (2007) a key partner in the world-famous innovative, advertising agency B.B.D.O., attributed the success of his company to eliminating criticism and negative feedback in group idea-generating sessions. He wrote in *Your Creative Power* that, "Creativity is so delicate a flower that praise tends to make it bloom while discouragement often nips it in the bud." A complimentary remark, public recognition or positive review may be even more beneficial for changing emotional culture. All people crave positive feedback and the warmth that comes with knowing that they are appreciated and celebrated where they work (Poh, 2016). A study carried out by Harvard Business School even found that employees want to feel that their input is valuable to the company more than they want a raise or promotion. When asked, staff responded that most of all, they want their presence to be noticed and appreciated (Sirota, Mischkind & Meltzer, 2006).

Conversely, stress is a well known creativity killer. A negative workplace climate is inhospitable to risk-taking – ultimately choking out the seeds of creativity (Epstein, 2016). A stressful or even depressing work environment doesn't give one the mood to think of doing things differently. The employee would only look forward to the end of the day. Attachment or emotional bonding is based on feeling safe and secure in relationships and in the working environment and this may be what employees need to excel in their roles.

Spatial Transformation

The day of the isolated cubicle for workers is outdated. While workers still need some space to be alone, the worker also needs places to both think and to support idea sharing. Despite the recent trend toward open office floor plans, a study by Adobe and Forrester Consulting found 60 percent of respondents said they are most creative in private environments. However, this did not mean cubicles, but alone time. That doesn't necessarily equate to solitary work, though: 30 percent of this group also said they were highly collaborative in these private spaces. Genever (2016) states that today's more progressive and innovative organizations are coming up with amazing office spaces that are designed to bring people together. Moving from a physical office or cubicle to a more flexible, open workplace that leverages technology to support the anywhere, anytime work environment is a shift for many organizations.

Google, Facebook, Box and Pixar lead the way in office space innovations, believed to be based on the idea that friendship formation is based on physical space and that people who were in proximity to each other during the day tended to become friends and later adopted similar attitudes which would include the acceptance of creativity and innovation. Another unusual and popular element to incorporate into the workplace is food. Google, for example, has restaurants, large cafeterias and small kitchens throughout their offices. People run into other workers in these places and conversations start, which leads to idea sharing, which lead to innovative solutions.

Some other examples for spatial transformational working environments include the following.

- Slides
- Outdoor Space
- Microsoft provides a comfortable seating area and huge touchscreen tablet for discussion, collaboration, and exploration.
- Epic has a hallway in their office that is designed to look like a subway.
- Infosys installed a bowling alley in one of their offices to allow employees to take a break and have some fun.
- Box installed swings in one area of their office so employees can swing while they chat and collaborate.

There are some common themes found in recommendations for innovative office spaces. These include an open plan and other design features (e.g., high-traffic staircases) that encourage accidental interactions, common areas than are strictly necessary- multiple cafeterias, other places to read and work that encourage workers to leave confined offices, Cemphasis on areas that hold two or more people, rather than single-occupancy offices and purpose-free generic "thinking" areas in open-plan spaces, which encourage workers to do their thinking in the presence of other people, rather than alone (Alter, n.d.). Workplace transformation occurs when real estate, technology, and human behaviors are leveraged to create fun, flexible, collaborative environments that foster innovation and enable a variety of work styles. For more innovative office space designs search Forbes innovative office spaces.

Figure 2. EMEA's engineering hub in Zurich, Switzerland
Photo courtesy of Glassdoor

Figure 3. Selgas Cano Architecture, Madrid
(http://hiconsumption.com/2014/02/selgas-cano-architecture-office-in-the-woods-of-madrid/)

Figure 4. Microsoft provides touchscreen tables
Photo courtesy of Glassdoor

Issues, Controversies, Problems: Reward Systems

Rewards: In the Eye of the Beholder

Extrinsic or intrinsic rewards, the debate continues as to how best to provide support for creativity in the working environment. There is some evidence to support both extrinsic and intrinsic rewards. Clearly, workers need money to survive and it unrealistic to assume extrinsic rewards do not impact work. Yet studies indicate that the need for intrinsic motivation is vital to the creative process (Amabile, 1996; Liu, et al., 2016; Mumford, 2003; Sternberg, 2006). The opportunity to contribute to the development and success of the workplace by generating creative ideas and implementing innovation seems to be more meaningful to individuals than monetary rewards (Rasulzada, 2014).

Extrinsic vs. Intrinsic Rewards

There have been many studies that indicate extrinsic rewards can have an undermining effect on intrinsic motivation which is one key component of creativity (Amabile, 1997; Baer, Olham, & Cummings, 2003; Burroughs, Dahl, Moreau, Chattopadhyay & Gorn, 2011; Deci, 1971; Deci & Ryan,1985; Eisenberger, & Shanock, 2003; Frey & Jegen, 2001; Lepper, Greene & Nisbett,

1973). Although studies indicate that providing employees with intrinsic rewards has the potential to enhance creative performance, many managers continue to emphasize the use of extrinsic rewards (e.g., monetary incentives and recognition) to stimulate their employees' creativity (Fairbank & Williams, 2001; Frese, Teng, & Wijnen, 1999; Van Dijk & Van den Ende, 2002).

There are some rewards that stimulate intrinsic motivation in the workplace. Several scholars have argued that high intrinsic motivation (i.e., the individual is excited about an activity and engages in it for the pleasure and satisfaction of solving problems) is the driving force behind creativity. Amabile (1996) maintains that extrinsically controlled factors stifle creativity. While extrinsic rewards are important rewards for the workforce, the act of creativity demands intrinsic motivation to develop and thrive. Intrinsic rewards come from motivation, curiosity in risk-free working environments and rewards that employees find stimulating.

Given these contradictory findings, research is needed that explores the specific circumstances under which extrinsic, contingent rewards have positive, neutral, or negative effects on creativity (Eisenberger & Cameron, 1996). The results of such research could help us better understand these earlier inconsistent findings while providing managers with a clear strategy for the optimal use of extrinsic rewards with respect to creativity.

Transformational Rewards

Managers should promote a safe, nonjudgmental atmosphere where new ideas are welcomed and failure not a punishable offense. Employees need to know there is support from individual, team, and cooperate learning. If you want to get employees to think out-of-the-box, you will need to motivate and support them with some form of rewards (Poh, 2016). All rewards for behavior do not necessarily need to be financial. In fact, a complimentary remark, public recognition or positive review may be even more beneficial for changing culture.

SOLUTIONS AND RECOMMENDATIONS: TRANSFORMING THE WORKPLACE INTO A REWARD SYSTEM

The workplace itself can serve as a reward system that supports intrinsic motivation. In earlier sections of this chapter the authors discussed the importance of psychosocial influences on the workplace and the unlimited options for spatial innovation to support the workers. Setting a more open, flexible environment can transform the workplace itself into a reward system. As well as earlier ideas about an environment to support creativity the following ideas can make any workplace more rewarding.

- **Solid Feedback:** People want to be recognized and praised for their ideas and hard work. This is all well and good, but it can be even more valuable if you offer feedback on what exactly you liked and what could possibly be worked on.
- **Value Flexibility:** Break the hold on 9-to-5 hours. Flexible multinational companies like Google allow developers to spend 20 percent of their working hours on side projects. Provide a variety of environments to give employees the flexibility to choose their work setting.
- **Build Confidence:** Creativity is personal. Create a safe environment in which there is no such thing as a bad idea and the quirky ideas are loved, encouraged and taken seriously. New ideas should always be recognized and rewarded.
- **Publicize Successes:** Success should be spread. For example, Multiview, a successful digital marketing firm features a 9th floor Newsletter and Wall of Fame that celebrates leading sales representatives. Create a simple trophy unique to the company. It does not have to be huge, just a token of appreciation and acknowledgement of creative thinking (Wahl, 2015).
- **Eliminate Public Criticism:** Alex Osborn, partner in the world famous B.B.D.O. advertising agency attributes the success of his company to eliminating criticism and negative feedback in group idea-generating sessions.
- **Encourage Curiosity:** Give people the freedom to explore uncharted territory and ideate. Creative inspiration can come from the most unlikely of places and sometimes when we step back from our professional environment.
- **Make Work Fun:** Having fun during work allows one to be relaxed and that's where one tends to get inspired with wonderful ideas. A stressful or even depressing work environment doesn't give one the mood to think of doing things differently. The employee would only look forward to the end of the day. Positive mood awards us with greater flexibility in thinking because our perspectives are widened (Bloomgarden, 2015).

- **Set Parameter:** Outside the box does not mean run amok but refers to being open-minded in that sense and are willing to explore alternatives. Creativity needs structure to flourish, but not so much structure that it is crushed.
- **Provide Access and Tools:** Make sure employees have access to all their data and applications wherever they are. This includes collaborative tools for group projects regardless of location. Allow employees to use their preferred device.

Ultimately, it is time for a new era in the workplace- an era of creativity that will redefine how organizations function. By reviewing the corporate culture and the office environment to place more emphasis on creativity, organizations are reaping the benefits and becoming leaders in their respective industries (Genever, 2016).

Recommendations for Growing Individual Creativity

The burden of stimulating creativity does not lie with the company alone. Individuals need to self-regulate their creativity transformation to better contribute to the group. Another component of this includes growing creative individuals in your workplace. Individuals can enhance their own creative thinking through a variety of activities. Epstein (2000) recommends that individuals:

- Capture your new ideas. Keep an idea notebook or voice recorder with you, type in new thoughts on your laptop or write ideas down on a napkin.
- Seek out challenging tasks. Take on projects that don't necessarily have a solution—such as trying to figure out how to make your dog fly or how to build a perfect model of the brain. This causes old ideas to compete, which helps generate new ones.
- Broaden your knowledge. Take a class outside psychology or read journals in unrelated fields, suggests Epstein. This makes more diverse knowledge available for interconnection, he says, which is the basis for all creative thought. "Ask for permission to sit in on lectures for a class on 12th century architecture and take notes," he suggests. "You'll do better in psychology and life if you broaden your knowledge."

Creative Transformation

- Surround yourself with interesting things and people. Regular dinners with diverse and interesting friends and a work space festooned with out-of-the-ordinary objects will help you develop more original ideas,
- Engage in outside activities. You can also keep your thoughts lively by taking a trip to an art museum or attending an opera—anything that stimulates new thinking.

FUTURE RESEARCH DIRECTIONS

There are some accepted premises about changing the workplace environment to support and sustain creativity, but there is limited information about how these environments influence different cultural groups or how one would change belief systems to accept and respect all contributors to optimize creative thinking. Making transformations, no matter how major, to the workplace is not the magic solution that will suddenly optimize all aspects of creativity. It is, however, a great step in the journey of fostering maximal creativity. Future research should seek empirical support to determine which aspects (or combinations of aspects) of the workplace are the most important to fostering creativity in the most workers possible. Flexibility may be the key- you want a place that fosters collaboration, but also allows for individual work time- a place that brings in unique elements, while still having access to some of the familiar elements that are needed to complete the traditional tasks that accompany work in all fields. The goal is to have a workplace that makes available those items and situations needed for employees to flourish. Considering that different employees have different needs at different times depending on specific task demands, this is no small challenge. Increased research and consideration into the most effective ways to promote creative transformation is needed and would be a productive endeavor.

Another area that needs investigation, in addition to the physical workspace is the mental workplace. Specifically, how should the need for emotional support in the workplace best be implemented? What types of training would managers need to address the needs of their workers? What should the role of co-workers be in the emotional support process? What ways can the physical environment contribute to the emotional support needs of employees and employers alike? Questions such as these need further investigation- as emotional support is a relatively new expectation of the current workforce that is likely to increase in future generations.

CONCLUSION

As hierarchies flatten and organizations become more networked, providing employees the ability to craft the environment that works best for them is critical to creating a highly functional workplace. Encouraging creativity is one of the most important things one can do as a leader. Create the space for everyone to think differently-to disrupt themselves, their business and the way they work (Bloomgarder, 2015). Creativity is a bigger predictor of success in life and work than intelligence. While most educational institutions and businesses still value intelligence over creativity the tide is turning and creativity must lead the way if the needed innovation for the creative age is to reach fruition (Poh, 2016). Creativity can be learned and nurtured when supported in the workplace. Creativity is the new literacy and a condition or skill that will be needed to thrive in the workplace.

In the forward, Dr. Williams indicates that creativity means survival of the workplace and workforce. As society evolves, survival of the fittest has evolved to survival of the most creative. In a world that demands flexible thinking, rapid and continuous change, the workplace that thrives demands creative innovation. Tomorrow brings many new challenges as the workplace transforms into the optimal environment to support creativity.

REFERENCES

Adobe Systems Incorporated. (2016). *State of Create Study*. Retrieved from http://www.adobe.com/content/dam/acom/en/max/pdfs/AdobeStateofCreate_2016_Report_Final.pdf

Alter, A. (n.d.). How to build a collaborative office space like Pixar and Google. *Iteration*. Retrieved from http://99u.com/articles/16408/how-to-build-a-collaborative-office-space-like-pixar-and-google

Andersson, A.E. & Stromquist, U. (1988). *K-samhallets framtid*. Stockholm: Prisma.

Amabile, T. M. (1997). Motivating creativity in organizations: On doing what you love and loving what you do. *California Management Review*, *40*(1), 39–58. doi:10.2307/41165921

Amabile, T. M. (1996). *Creativity in context*. Boulder, CO: Westview Press.

Baer, M., Oldham, G. R., & Cummings, A. (2003). Rewarding creativity: When does it matter? *The Leadership Quarterly, 14*(4-5), 569–586. doi:10.1016/S1048-9843(03)00052-3

Bloomgarden, K. (2015). How to reward good (and bad) ideas at work. *Fortune Insiders*. Retrieved from http://fortune.com/2015/08/19/kathy-bloomgarden-importance-of-creativity-in-the-workplace/

Burroughs, J. E., Dahl, D. W., Moreau, C. P., Chattopadhyay, A., & Gorn, G. J. (2011). Facilitating and rewarding creativity during new product development. *Journal of Marketing, 75*(4), 53–67. doi:10.1509/jmkg.75.4.53

Cher, B. (2015). The workplace of the future: Reality vs myth. *Digital News Asia*. Retrieved from https://www.digitalnewsasia.com/workplace-future-reality-vs-myth

Chiswick Consulting. (2015). *Why offering emotional support in the workplace can lead to increased productivity*. Retrieved from http://www.chiswickconsulting.com/why-offering-emotional-support-in-the-workplace-can-lead-to-increased-productivity/

Deci, E. L. (1971). Effects of externally mediated rewards on intrinsic motivation. *Journal of Personality and Social Psychology, 18*, 105–115. doi:10.1037/h0030644

Deci, E. L. (1971). Effects of externally mediated rewards on intrinsic motivation. *Journal of Personality and Social Psychology, 18*(1), 105–115. doi:10.1037/h0030644

Deci, E. L., & Ryan, R. M. (1985). *Intrinsic motivation and self-determination in human behavior*. New York: Plenum. doi:10.1007/978-1-4899-2271-7

Eisenberger, R., & Cameron, J. (1996). Detrimental effects of reward: Reality or myth? *The American Psychologist, 51*(11), 1153–1166. doi:10.1037/0003-066X.51.11.1153 PMID:8937264

Eisenberger, R., & Shanock, L. (2003). Rewards, intrinsic motivation and creativity: A case study of conceptual and methodological isolation. *Creativity Research Journal, 15*(2-3), 121–130. doi:10.1080/10400419.2003.9651404

Epstein, R. (2000). *The big book of creativity games*. New York: McGraw-Hill.

Epstein, R. (2016). *How to foster creativity in the workplace.* Retrieved from http://multiview.com/associations/resources/how-to-foster-creativity-in-the-workplace

Fairbank, J. F., & Williams, S. D. (2001). Motivating creativity and enhancing innovation through employee suggestion system technology. *Creativity and Innovation Management, 10*(2), 68–74. doi:10.1111/1467-8691.00204

Fallon, N. (2014). Why creativity matters most for entrepreneurs. *Business News Daily.* Retrieved from http://www.businessnewsdaily.com/5813-creativity-in-entrepreneurship.html

Fallon, N. (2016). How crucial is creativity to your business success? *Business News Daily.* Retrieved from http://www.businessnewsdaily.com/8894-creativity-business-success.html

Florida, R. L. (2004). *The rise of the creative class: And how it's transforming work, leisure, community and everyday life.* New York: Basic Books.

Florida, R. L. (2012). *The psychology behind why creative people cluster. The Rise of the Creative Class, Revisited.* New York: Basic Books.

Florida, R. L., & Knudson, B. (2004) *Beyond Spillovers.* Retrieved from http://www.citylab.com/housing/2012/07/psychology-behind-why-creative-people-cluster/2243/

Frey, B. S., & Jegen, R. (2001). Motivation crowding theory. *Journal of Economic Surveys, 15*(5), 589–611. doi:10.1111/1467-6419.00150

Frese, M., Teng, E., & Wijnen, C. J. (1999). Helping to improve suggestion systems: Predictors of making suggestions in companies. *Journal of Organizational Behavior, 20*(7), 1139–1155. doi:10.1002/(SICI)1099-1379(199912)20:7<1139::AID-JOB946>3.0.CO;2-I

Gendron, R. (2017). *5 tips for a creative workplace.* Association for Talent Development. Retrieved from https://www.td.org/Publications/Blogs/Human-Capital-Blog/2017/01/5-Tips-for-a-Creative-Workplace

Genever, H. (2016). 4 ways to cultivate workplace creativity. *Lifeplan.* Retrieved from https://www.liveplan.com/blog/2016/06/4-ways-to-cultivate-workplace-creativity-a-liveplan-guide/

Hansen, H. K. (2008). *The urban turn – and the location of economic activities. Meddelanden fran Lunds Universitets Geografiska Institution, Avhandlingar CLXXVI.* Lund University.

Hoff, E. (2014). The creative place: the impact of different environmental factors on creativity. In E. Shiu (Ed.), *Creativity Research.* London: Routledge.

JobsS. (n.d.). Retrieved from https://www.brainyquote.com/quotes/authors/s/steve_jobs.html

Jobs, S. (1982). *Steve Jobs speech at Golden Plate Awards.* Academy of Achievement Speech. Retrieved from https://genius.com/Steve-jobs-academy-of-achievement-speech-1982-annotated

Lepper, M. R., Greene, D., & Nisbett, R. E. (1973). Undermining childrens intrinsic interest with extrinsic reward: A test of over justification hypothesis. *Journal of Personality and Social Psychology, 28*(1), 129–137. doi:10.1037/h0035519

Liu, D., Jiang, K., Shalley, C. E., Keem, S., & Zhou, J. (2016). Motivational mechanisms of employee creativity: A meta-analytic examination and theoretical extension of the creativity literature. *Organizational Behavior and Human Decision Processes, 137,* 236–263. doi:10.1016/j.obhdp.2016.08.001

Mumford, M. D. (2003). Where have we been, where are we going? Taking stock in creativity research. *Creativity Research Journal, 15*(2-3), 107–120. doi:10.1080/10400419.2003.9651403

Niedomysl, T. (2010). Towards a conceptual framework of place attractiveness: A migration perspective. *Geografiska Annaler. Series B, Human Geography, 92*(1), 97–109. doi:10.1111/j.1468-0467.2010.00335.x

Noone, J. (2010). The lion and the ant story: Some lessons for HR and managers. *One World.* Retrieved from https://josephnoone.com/2010/05/08/the-lion-and-the-ant-some-lessons-for-managers-and-hr/

Olmstead, K., Lampe, C., & Ellison, N. B. (2016). *Social media and the workplace.* Retrieved from http://www.pewinternet.org/2016/06/22/social-media-and-the-workplace/

Osborn, A. (2007). *Your creative power.* New York: Charles Scribner's Sons.

PEW Research Center. (2014). Retrieved from http://www.pewinternet.org/2016/06/22/social-media-and-the-workplace/pi_2016-06-22_social-media-and-work_0-02/

Poh, M. (2016). *Six ways to unleash creativity in the workplace.* Retrieved from http://www.hongkiat.com/blog/unleash-creativity-workplace/

Rasulzada, F. (2014). Creativity at work and its relation to well-being. In E. Shiu (Ed.), *Creativity Research.* London: Routledge.

Sirota, D., Mischkind, L. A., & Meltzer, M. I. (2006). *Why your employees are losing motivation.* Harvard Business School. Retrieved from http://hbswk.hbs.edu/archive/5289.html

Sternberg, R. J. (2006). The nature of creativity. *Creativity Research Journal, 18*(1), 87–98. doi:10.1207/s15326934crj1801_10

Tai, H. T., & Mai, N. Q. (2016). Proactive personality, organizational context, employee creativity and innovative capability: Evidence from MNCs and domestic corporations. *The International Journal of Organizational Analysis, 24*(3), 370–389. doi:10.1108/IJOA-04-2015-0857

Taylor, N. F. (2016). How crucial is creativity to your business success? *Business News Daily.* Retrieved from http://www.businessnewsdaily.com/8894-creativity-business-success.html

Van Dijk, C., & Van Den Ende, J. (2002). Suggestion systems: Transferring employee creativity into practicable ideas. *R & D Management, 32*(5), 387–395. doi:10.1111/1467-9310.00270

Wahl, E. (2015). How to encourage and reward creativity in the workplace. *How to Human Resources.* Retrieved from http://www.bizjournals.com/bizjournals/how-to/human-resources/2015/09/how-to-encourage-and-reward-creativity.html

Related Readings

To continue IGI Global's long-standing tradition of advancing innovation through emerging research, please find below a compiled list of recommended IGI Global book chapters and journal articles in the areas of workforce development, team building, and employability. These related readings will provide additional information and guidance to further enrich your knowledge and assist you with your own research.

Adada, N., Shatila, A., & Mneymneh, N. M. (2017). Technology Leadership: Bridging the Gap between Problems and Solutions in Lebanese Schools. In R. Styron Jr & J. Styron (Eds.), *Comprehensive Problem-Solving and Skill Development for Next-Generation Leaders* (pp. 293–312). Hershey, PA: IGI Global. doi:10.4018/978-1-5225-1968-3.ch014

Ahmed, A. A., Witte, M. M., & Witte, J. E. (2014). Education in Egypt and its Role in the Global Community. In V. Wang (Ed.), *International Education and the Next-Generation Workforce: Competition in the Global Economy* (pp. 83–99). Hershey, PA: IGI Global. doi:10.4018/978-1-4666-4498-4.ch005

Angelova, R. A. (2017). Cross-Cultural Management of the European Textile and Clothing Industries: Application of Hofstede's Cultural Dimensions. In B. Christiansen & H. Chandan (Eds.), *Handbook of Research on Organizational Culture and Diversity in the Modern Workforce* (pp. 239–260). Hershey, PA: IGI Global. doi:10.4018/978-1-5225-2250-8.ch011

Atiku, S. O., & Fields, Z. (2017). Multicultural Orientations for 21st Century Global Leadership. In N. Baporikar (Ed.), *Management Education for Global Leadership* (pp. 28–51). Hershey, PA: IGI Global. doi:10.4018/978-1-5225-1013-0.ch002

Avni, E., & Rotem, A. (2016). Digital Competence: A Net of Literacies. In Y. Rosen, S. Ferrara, & M. Mosharraf (Eds.), *Handbook of Research on Technology Tools for Real-World Skill Development* (pp. 13–41). Hershey, PA: IGI Global. doi:10.4018/978-1-4666-9441-5.ch002

Back, S. M., Greenhalgh-Spencer, H., & Frias, K. M. (2016). The Application of Transdisciplinary Theory and Practice to STEM Education. In Y. Rosen, S. Ferrara, & M. Mosharraf (Eds.), *Handbook of Research on Technology Tools for Real-World Skill Development* (pp. 42–67). Hershey, PA: IGI Global. doi:10.4018/978-1-4666-9441-5.ch003

Baporikar, N. (2017). Global Perspective on Talent Management: The South African Experience. In M. Mupepi (Ed.), *Effective Talent Management Strategies for Organizational Success* (pp. 283–300). Hershey, PA: IGI Global. doi:10.4018/978-1-5225-1961-4.ch018

Baporikar, N. (2017). Learner Centred Approach for Global Leadership in Management Education. In N. Baporikar (Ed.), *Management Education for Global Leadership* (pp. 202–220). Hershey, PA: IGI Global. doi:10.4018/978-1-5225-1013-0.ch010

Baptiste, L., & Moss, T. (2017). A British and Dutch Caribbean Overseas Territories Training Evaluation Case Study: An HIV/AIDS Workforce Training Perspective. In S. Frasard & F. Prasuhn (Eds.), *Training Initiatives and Strategies for the Modern Workforce* (pp. 19–40). Hershey, PA: IGI Global. doi:10.4018/978-1-5225-1808-2.ch002

Barrons, K. P., & McGinnis, T. C. (2017). Building Capability: Flipping the Zone of Proximal Development For Talent Management. In M. Mupepi (Ed.), *Effective Talent Management Strategies for Organizational Success* (pp. 160–176). Hershey, PA: IGI Global. doi:10.4018/978-1-5225-1961-4.ch011

Benton, C. J., White, O. L., & Stratton, S. K. (2014). Collaboration Not Competition: International Education Expanding Perspectives on Learning and Workforce Articulation. In V. Wang (Ed.), *International Education and the Next-Generation Workforce: Competition in the Global Economy* (pp. 64–82). Hershey, PA: IGI Global. doi:10.4018/978-1-4666-4498-4.ch004

Billington, R. (2017). A Critique on the Factors that Influence Mental Health Workforce Training in Developing Countries. In M. Smith & A. Jury (Eds.), *Workforce Development Theory and Practice in the Mental Health Sector* (pp. 130–143). Hershey, PA: IGI Global. doi:10.4018/978-1-5225-1874-7.ch006

Related Readings

Bingham, H. M. (2017). Undergraduate Nursing Curriculum Content Focuses on Emerging Issues that Influence Health. In M. Smith & A. Jury (Eds.), *Workforce Development Theory and Practice in the Mental Health Sector* (pp. 182–199). Hershey, PA: IGI Global. doi:10.4018/978-1-5225-1874-7.ch009

Bishop, J. (2017). Detecting Sexual Harassment in Workplace Electronic Communications Networks: The Role of "PROTEGER" for Augmentive Behaviour Monitoring. In B. Christiansen & H. Chandan (Eds.), *Handbook of Research on Organizational Culture and Diversity in the Modern Workforce* (pp. 181–216). Hershey, PA: IGI Global. doi:10.4018/978-1-5225-2250-8.ch009

Bridgeforth, J. S. (2017). Multicultural Leadership in Higher Education. In R. Styron Jr & J. Styron (Eds.), *Comprehensive Problem-Solving and Skill Development for Next-Generation Leaders* (pp. 139–164). Hershey, PA: IGI Global. doi:10.4018/978-1-5225-1968-3.ch007

Byrd, M. Y., & Hughes, C. (2015). A Paradigm Shift for Diversity Management: From Promoting Business Opportunity to Optimizing Lived Career Work Experiences. In C. Hughes (Ed.), *Impact of Diversity on Organization and Career Development* (pp. 28–53). Hershey, PA: IGI Global. doi:10.4018/978-1-4666-7324-3.ch002

Chakraborty, M., & Wang, J. (2015). The Postmodern Approach to Career Counseling for Contemporary Organizations. In C. Hughes (Ed.), *Impact of Diversity on Organization and Career Development* (pp. 252–274). Hershey, PA: IGI Global. doi:10.4018/978-1-4666-7324-3.ch010

Cicerali, E. E., & Cicerali, L. K. (2017). Workplace Incivility as Low-Level Violence: Theories, Consequences, and Future Research Suggestions. In B. Christiansen & H. Chandan (Eds.), *Handbook of Research on Organizational Culture and Diversity in the Modern Workforce* (pp. 155–180). Hershey, PA: IGI Global. doi:10.4018/978-1-5225-2250-8.ch008

Claver-Cortés, E., & Fernández-Sánchez, J. A. (2017). Staff Restructuring: Old Methods, New Challenges. *International Journal of Innovation in the Digital Economy*, 8(1), 1–18. doi:10.4018/IJIDE.2017010101

Coombs, T., Burgess, P., Dickson, R., & McKay, R. (2017). Routine Outcome Measurement and the Development of the Australian Mental Health Workforce: The First 25 Years of Implementation Are the Hardest. In M. Smith & A. Jury (Eds.), *Workforce Development Theory and Practice in the Mental Health Sector* (pp. 302–316). Hershey, PA: IGI Global. doi:10.4018/978-1-5225-1874-7.ch015

Cordeiro, C. M. (2017). Relativity in Perspective in Culture Theories: The Götheborg IV Model. In B. Christiansen & H. Chandan (Eds.), *Handbook of Research on Organizational Culture and Diversity in the Modern Workforce* (pp. 217–238). Hershey, PA: IGI Global. doi:10.4018/978-1-5225-2250-8.ch010

Daves, D. P. (2017). Principles of Effective Leadership. In R. Styron Jr & J. Styron (Eds.), *Comprehensive Problem-Solving and Skill Development for Next-Generation Leaders* (pp. 40–56). Hershey, PA: IGI Global. doi:10.4018/978-1-5225-1968-3.ch002

Delmas, P. M. (2017). Research-Based Leadership for Next-Generation Leaders. In R. Styron Jr & J. Styron (Eds.), *Comprehensive Problem-Solving and Skill Development for Next-Generation Leaders* (pp. 1–39). Hershey, PA: IGI Global. doi:10.4018/978-1-5225-1968-3.ch001

Deng, Y. (2017). Managing Talent in Global Environments: Effective Communication in Multinational Enterprise. In M. Mupepi (Ed.), *Effective Talent Management Strategies for Organizational Success* (pp. 235–259). Hershey, PA: IGI Global. doi:10.4018/978-1-5225-1961-4.ch016

Deshpande, M. (2017). Best Practices in Management Institutions for Global Leadership: Policy Aspects. In N. Baporikar (Ed.), *Management Education for Global Leadership* (pp. 1–27). Hershey, PA: IGI Global. doi:10.4018/978-1-5225-1013-0.ch001

Donovan, P. (2017). Finding the Critical Few: The Hot Buttons of Training Transfer at ICON – A Case Study in Evaluation and Learning Transfer at a Global CRO (Clinical Research Organization). In S. Frasard & F. Prasuhn (Eds.), *Training Initiatives and Strategies for the Modern Workforce* (pp. 127–157). Hershey, PA: IGI Global. doi:10.4018/978-1-5225-1808-2.ch007

Related Readings

Duran, A., & Lopez, D. (2015). Women from Diverse Backgrounds in the Science, Technology, Engineering, and Math (STEM) Professions: Retention and Career Development. In C. Hughes (Ed.), *Impact of Diversity on Organization and Career Development* (pp. 214–251). Hershey, PA: IGI Global. doi:10.4018/978-1-4666-7324-3.ch009

Eckardt, P., Janotha, B., Marino, M. A., Erlanger, D. P., & Cannella, D. (2016). Equipping Advanced Practice Nurses with Real-World Skills. In Y. Rosen, S. Ferrara, & M. Mosharraf (Eds.), *Handbook of Research on Technology Tools for Real-World Skill Development* (pp. 163–189). Hershey, PA: IGI Global. doi:10.4018/978-1-4666-9441-5.ch007

Efeoğlu, E. I., & Ozcan, S. (2017). The Relationship Between Social Problem Solving Ability and Burnout Level: A Field Study Among Health Professionals. In B. Christiansen & H. Chandan (Eds.), *Handbook of Research on Human Factors in Contemporary Workforce Development* (pp. 268–282). Hershey, PA: IGI Global. doi:10.4018/978-1-5225-2568-4.ch012

Efeoğlu, E. I., & Pekkan, N. U. (2017). The Relationship Between Employee Empowerment and Organizational Cynicism: An Implementation in the Banking Sector. In B. Christiansen & H. Chandan (Eds.), *Handbook of Research on Organizational Culture and Diversity in the Modern Workforce* (pp. 309–322). Hershey, PA: IGI Global. doi:10.4018/978-1-5225-2250-8.ch014

Elazier, T. (2017). Successful Evaluation by Design. In S. Frasard & F. Prasuhn (Eds.), *Training Initiatives and Strategies for the Modern Workforce* (pp. 1–18). Hershey, PA: IGI Global. doi:10.4018/978-1-5225-1808-2.ch001

Ellington, L. (2014). Critical Teaching and Learning Issues in International Education. In V. Wang (Ed.), *International Education and the Next-Generation Workforce: Competition in the Global Economy* (pp. 100–114). Hershey, PA: IGI Global. doi:10.4018/978-1-4666-4498-4.ch006

Elufiede, O. J., & Flynn, B. B. (2017). Mentor the Leader: A Transformational Approach. In R. Styron Jr & J. Styron (Eds.), *Comprehensive Problem-Solving and Skill Development for Next-Generation Leaders* (pp. 188–209). Hershey, PA: IGI Global. doi:10.4018/978-1-5225-1968-3.ch009

Elzarka, S., Beltran, V., Decker, J. C., Matzaganian, M., & Walker, N. T. (2016). The Value of Metacognition and Reflectivity in Computer-Based Learning Environments. In Y. Rosen, S. Ferrara, & M. Mosharraf (Eds.), *Handbook of Research on Technology Tools for Real-World Skill Development* (pp. 105–136). Hershey, PA: IGI Global. doi:10.4018/978-1-4666-9441-5.ch005

Estis, J. M. (2017). Changing Culture through Active Learning. In R. Styron Jr & J. Styron (Eds.), *Comprehensive Problem-Solving and Skill Development for Next-Generation Leaders* (pp. 96–115). Hershey, PA: IGI Global. doi:10.4018/978-1-5225-1968-3.ch005

Farmer, L. S. (2014). The Roles of Professional Organizations in School Library Education. In V. Wang (Ed.), *International Education and the Next-Generation Workforce: Competition in the Global Economy* (pp. 170–193). Hershey, PA: IGI Global. doi:10.4018/978-1-4666-4498-4.ch010

Ferrari, F. (2017). Human Resource Management and Organizational Reliability: Coordination Mechanisms, Training Models, and Diagnostic Systems for Contingency Management. In B. Christiansen & H. Chandan (Eds.), *Handbook of Research on Organizational Culture and Diversity in the Modern Workforce* (pp. 43–59). Hershey, PA: IGI Global. doi:10.4018/978-1-5225-2250-8.ch003

Fisher, H. B., & Spikes, W. F. (2017). Examining the Relationship Between Learning, Continuing Legal Education, and the Improvement of the Practice of the Law. In S. Frasard & F. Prasuhn (Eds.), *Training Initiatives and Strategies for the Modern Workforce* (pp. 90–115). Hershey, PA: IGI Global. doi:10.4018/978-1-5225-1808-2.ch005

Giannouli, V. (2017). Emotional Aspects of Leadership in the Modern Workplace. In B. Christiansen & H. Chandan (Eds.), *Handbook of Research on Human Factors in Contemporary Workforce Development* (pp. 24–59). Hershey, PA: IGI Global. doi:10.4018/978-1-5225-2568-4.ch002

Green, W. S. (2017). Increasing Leadership Capacity through Emotional Intelligence. In R. Styron Jr & J. Styron (Eds.), *Comprehensive Problem-Solving and Skill Development for Next-Generation Leaders* (pp. 57–75). Hershey, PA: IGI Global. doi:10.4018/978-1-5225-1968-3.ch003

Related Readings

Greenfield, M. (2017). Perspectives on the Historical Evolution of the People Side of Business. In B. Christiansen & H. Chandan (Eds.), *Handbook of Research on Organizational Culture and Diversity in the Modern Workforce* (pp. 1–22). Hershey, PA: IGI Global. doi:10.4018/978-1-5225-2250-8.ch001

Guilott, M. C., Parker, G. A., & Wheat, C. A. (2017). Tools to Change School Culture: Learning About Learning Together. In R. Styron Jr & J. Styron (Eds.), *Comprehensive Problem-Solving and Skill Development for Next-Generation Leaders* (pp. 165–186). Hershey, PA: IGI Global. doi:10.4018/978-1-5225-1968-3.ch008

Gupton, S. L. (2017). Technology's Impact on Higher Education: Implications for next Generation Leaders. In R. Styron Jr & J. Styron (Eds.), *Comprehensive Problem-Solving and Skill Development for Next-Generation Leaders* (pp. 278–292). Hershey, PA: IGI Global. doi:10.4018/978-1-5225-1968-3.ch013

Harmes, J. C., Welsh, J. L., & Winkelman, R. J. (2016). A Framework for Defining and Evaluating Technology Integration in the Instruction of Real-World Skills. In Y. Rosen, S. Ferrara, & M. Mosharraf (Eds.), *Handbook of Research on Technology Tools for Real-World Skill Development* (pp. 137–162). Hershey, PA: IGI Global. doi:10.4018/978-1-4666-9441-5.ch006

Hendel, R. J. (2017). Leadership for Improving Student Success through Higher Cognitive Instruction. In R. Styron Jr & J. Styron (Eds.), *Comprehensive Problem-Solving and Skill Development for Next-Generation Leaders* (pp. 230–254). Hershey, PA: IGI Global. doi:10.4018/978-1-5225-1968-3.ch011

Hennessy, J. L., Smythe, L., Abbott, M., & Hughes, F. A. (2017). Mental Health Support Workers: An Evolving Workforce. In M. Smith & A. Jury (Eds.), *Workforce Development Theory and Practice in the Mental Health Sector* (pp. 200–221). Hershey, PA: IGI Global. doi:10.4018/978-1-5225-1874-7.ch010

Henschke, J. A. (2014). Observations of the Possible Influence of Andragogy on the Economies of World Nations. In V. Wang (Ed.), *International Education and the Next-Generation Workforce: Competition in the Global Economy* (pp. 115–138). Hershey, PA: IGI Global. doi:10.4018/978-1-4666-4498-4.ch007

Hieker, C., & Rushby, M. (2017). Diversity in the Workplace: How to Achieve Gender Diversity in the Workplace. In B. Christiansen & H. Chandan (Eds.), *Handbook of Research on Human Factors in Contemporary Workforce Development* (pp. 308–332). Hershey, PA: IGI Global. doi:10.4018/978-1-5225-2568-4.ch014

Hill, C. W., & Withy, K. (2017). Rural Mental Health Workforce Development in Hawai'i and the US-Affiliated Pacific Islands. In M. Smith & A. Jury (Eds.), *Workforce Development Theory and Practice in the Mental Health Sector* (pp. 60–89). Hershey, PA: IGI Global. doi:10.4018/978-1-5225-1874-7.ch003

Hoge, M. A., Stuart, G. W., Morris, J. A., Huey, L. Y., Flaherty, M. T., & Paris, M. Jr. (2017). Behavioral Health Workforce Development in the United States. In M. Smith & A. Jury (Eds.), *Workforce Development Theory and Practice in the Mental Health Sector* (pp. 37–59). Hershey, PA: IGI Global. doi:10.4018/978-1-5225-1874-7.ch002

Hughes, C. (2015). Integrating Diversity into Organization and Career Development: A Changing Perspective. In C. Hughes (Ed.), *Impact of Diversity on Organization and Career Development* (pp. 1–27). Hershey, PA: IGI Global. doi:10.4018/978-1-4666-7324-3.ch001

Hughes, C. (2015). Leveraging Diversity for Competitive Advantage. In C. Hughes (Ed.), *Impact of Diversity on Organization and Career Development* (pp. 275–298). Hershey, PA: IGI Global. doi:10.4018/978-1-4666-7324-3.ch011

Hurst, R. R., Lloyd, J. T., & Miller, J. C. (2017). Raising the Bar: Moving Evaluation of Training From the Classroom Into the Business. In S. Frasard & F. Prasuhn (Eds.), *Training Initiatives and Strategies for the Modern Workforce* (pp. 41–60). Hershey, PA: IGI Global. doi:10.4018/978-1-5225-1808-2.ch003

Islam, S. M., Tabassum, R., Colet, P. C., Cruz, J. P., Dey, S., Rawal, L. B., & Islam, A. (2017). Human Resources for Mental Health in Low and Middle Income Countries: Evidence from Bangladesh. In M. Smith & A. Jury (Eds.), *Workforce Development Theory and Practice in the Mental Health Sector* (pp. 144–164). Hershey, PA: IGI Global. doi:10.4018/978-1-5225-1874-7.ch007

James, S., & Hauli, E. (2017). Holistic Management Education at Tanzanian Rural Development Planning Institute. In N. Baporikar (Ed.), *Management Education for Global Leadership* (pp. 112–136). Hershey, PA: IGI Global. doi:10.4018/978-1-5225-1013-0.ch006

Javaid, M. U., Isha, A. S., Nubling, M., Mirza, M. Z., & Ghazali, Z. (2017). Human Factors in Context to Occupational Health and Wellbeing. In B. Christiansen & H. Chandan (Eds.), *Handbook of Research on Organizational Culture and Diversity in the Modern Workforce* (pp. 60–77). Hershey, PA: IGI Global. doi:10.4018/978-1-5225-2250-8.ch004

Jiang, E. P. (2014). A Comparative Study on Undergraduate Computer Science Education between China and the United States. In V. Wang (Ed.), *International Education and the Next-Generation Workforce: Competition in the Global Economy* (pp. 208–223). Hershey, PA: IGI Global. doi:10.4018/978-1-4666-4498-4.ch012

Kamasak, R., Kar, A., Yavuz, M., & Baykut, S. (2017). Qualitative Methods in Organizational Research: An Example of Grounded Theory Data Analysis. In B. Christiansen & H. Chandan (Eds.), *Handbook of Research on Organizational Culture and Diversity in the Modern Workforce* (pp. 23–42). Hershey, PA: IGI Global. doi:10.4018/978-1-5225-2250-8.ch002

Kannabiran, G., Sarata, A., & Nagarani, M. (2016). Career Anchors and Employee Retention: An Empirical Study of Information Technology Industry in India. *International Journal of Knowledge-Based Organizations*, 6(3), 58–75. doi:10.4018/IJKBO.2016070104

Karapinar, P. B., & Camgoz, S. M. (2017). Well-Being at Work: A Comprehensive Review About Its Predictors and Outcomes. In B. Christiansen & H. Chandan (Eds.), *Handbook of Research on Organizational Culture and Diversity in the Modern Workforce* (pp. 78–99). Hershey, PA: IGI Global. doi:10.4018/978-1-5225-2250-8.ch005

Kasemsap, K. (2017). Exploring the Role of Organizational Culture in Modern Organizations. In R. Styron Jr & J. Styron (Eds.), *Comprehensive Problem-Solving and Skill Development for Next-Generation Leaders* (pp. 116–138). Hershey, PA: IGI Global. doi:10.4018/978-1-5225-1968-3.ch006

Kasemsap, K. (2017). Exploring the Role of Organizational Justice in the Modern Workplace. In B. Christiansen & H. Chandan (Eds.), *Handbook of Research on Organizational Culture and Diversity in the Modern Workforce* (pp. 323–345). Hershey, PA: IGI Global. doi:10.4018/978-1-5225-2250-8.ch015

Kasemsap, K. (2017). Fundamentals of Talent Management: Capitalizing on Intellectual Assets. In M. Mupepi (Ed.), *Effective Talent Management Strategies for Organizational Success* (pp. 260–282). Hershey, PA: IGI Global. doi:10.4018/978-1-5225-1961-4.ch017

Kasemsap, K. (2017). Mastering Employee Turnover Intention in the Modern Workforce. In B. Christiansen & H. Chandan (Eds.), *Handbook of Research on Organizational Culture and Diversity in the Modern Workforce* (pp. 382–401). Hershey, PA: IGI Global. doi:10.4018/978-1-5225-2250-8.ch018

Kasemsap, K. (2017). The Fundamentals of Organizational Citizenship Behavior. In B. Christiansen & H. Chandan (Eds.), *Handbook of Research on Human Factors in Contemporary Workforce Development* (pp. 1–23). Hershey, PA: IGI Global. doi:10.4018/978-1-5225-2568-4.ch001

Kasemsap, K. (2017). The Significance of Job Satisfaction in Modern Organizations. In B. Christiansen & H. Chandan (Eds.), *Handbook of Research on Human Factors in Contemporary Workforce Development* (pp. 181–200). Hershey, PA: IGI Global. doi:10.4018/978-1-5225-2568-4.ch008

Knox, C. H., Anderson-Inman, L., Terrazas-Arellanes, F. E., Walden, E. D., & Hildreth, B. (2016). The SOAR Strategies for Online Academic Research: Helping Middle School Students Meet New Standards. In Y. Rosen, S. Ferrara, & M. Mosharraf (Eds.), *Handbook of Research on Technology Tools for Real-World Skill Development* (pp. 68–104). Hershey, PA: IGI Global. doi:10.4018/978-1-4666-9441-5.ch004

Koech, J. K., & Pak, K. S. (2017). Using Training Evaluation to Improve Practice: A Lesson Learnt from Rolling Out LMS Upgrade Training. In S. Frasard & F. Prasuhn (Eds.), *Training Initiatives and Strategies for the Modern Workforce* (pp. 158–168). Hershey, PA: IGI Global. doi:10.4018/978-1-5225-1808-2.ch008

Koning, A., & Poole, S. J. (2017). Supporting People Who Experience Co-Existing Mental Health and Addiction Problems: A National Approach to Improving Responsiveness in Aotearoa New Zealand. In M. Smith & A. Jury (Eds.), *Workforce Development Theory and Practice in the Mental Health Sector* (pp. 251–270). Hershey, PA: IGI Global. doi:10.4018/978-1-5225-1874-7.ch012

Related Readings

Konyu-Fogel, G. (2015). Career Management and Human Resource Development of a Global, Diverse Workforce. In C. Hughes (Ed.), *Impact of Diversity on Organization and Career Development* (pp. 80–104). Hershey, PA: IGI Global. doi:10.4018/978-1-4666-7324-3.ch004

Kumar, R., & Jha, V. (2017). Traits of Leaders and Active Listening: A Theory. In B. Christiansen & H. Chandan (Eds.), *Handbook of Research on Organizational Culture and Diversity in the Modern Workforce* (pp. 364–381). Hershey, PA: IGI Global. doi:10.4018/978-1-5225-2250-8.ch017

Labat, M. B., Eadens, D. W., Labat, C. A., & Eadens, D. M. (2017). Motivational Factors for Pursuing Degrees in Educational Administration. In R. Styron Jr & J. Styron (Eds.), *Comprehensive Problem-Solving and Skill Development for Next-Generation Leaders* (pp. 210–228). Hershey, PA: IGI Global. doi:10.4018/978-1-5225-1968-3.ch010

Lawson, R., & Dunnachie, B. (2017). Workforce Development in the Child and Adolescent Mental Health Sector: The Challenge of Rolling out a Specialist Eating Disorders Treatment in New Zealand. In M. Smith & A. Jury (Eds.), *Workforce Development Theory and Practice in the Mental Health Sector* (pp. 271–283). Hershey, PA: IGI Global. doi:10.4018/978-1-5225-1874-7.ch013

Leonard, E. E. (2017). 21st Century Educational Leadership. In R. Styron Jr & J. Styron (Eds.), *Comprehensive Problem-Solving and Skill Development for Next-Generation Leaders* (pp. 313–332). Hershey, PA: IGI Global. doi:10.4018/978-1-5225-1968-3.ch015

Long, C. S. (2017). The Relationship Between Work-Life Balance (WLB) and Firm Performance. In B. Christiansen & H. Chandan (Eds.), *Handbook of Research on Organizational Culture and Diversity in the Modern Workforce* (pp. 402–411). Hershey, PA: IGI Global. doi:10.4018/978-1-5225-2250-8.ch019

Martin, S. J., & Reed, P. A. (2015). Instructional Alignment of Workplace Readiness Skills in Marketing Education. *International Journal of Adult Vocational Education and Technology*, 6(3), 31–44. doi:10.4018/IJAVET.2015070103

Matuska, E. M., & Grubicka, J. (2017). Employer Branding and Internet Security. In B. Christiansen & H. Chandan (Eds.), *Handbook of Research on Human Factors in Contemporary Workforce Development* (pp. 357–378). Hershey, PA: IGI Global. doi:10.4018/978-1-5225-2568-4.ch016

Maxey, E. C., & Moore, J. R. (2017). Impetus for Culture Transformation: Pre-Hire Training for Employees with Disabilities. In S. Frasard & F. Prasuhn (Eds.), *Training Initiatives and Strategies for the Modern Workforce* (pp. 116–126). Hershey, PA: IGI Global. doi:10.4018/978-1-5225-1808-2.ch006

McFadden, C., Maahs-Fladung, C., Mallett, W., & Zhao, L. (2014). Implications for Recruiting International Students to the University of North Carolina System. In V. Wang (Ed.), *International Education and the Next-Generation Workforce: Competition in the Global Economy* (pp. 139–153). Hershey, PA: IGI Global. doi:10.4018/978-1-4666-4498-4.ch008

McKay, R., Coombs, T., & Anderson, J. M. (2017). Mental Health and Addiction Workforce Development in Australia: Never the Twain to Meet? In M. Smith & A. Jury (Eds.), *Workforce Development Theory and Practice in the Mental Health Sector* (pp. 90–105). Hershey, PA: IGI Global. doi:10.4018/978-1-5225-1874-7.ch004

McLaughlin, G. (2017). The Impacts a Learner Response System Can Have in the Classroom. In S. Frasard & F. Prasuhn (Eds.), *Training Initiatives and Strategies for the Modern Workforce* (pp. 61–89). Hershey, PA: IGI Global. doi:10.4018/978-1-5225-1808-2.ch004

McLoughlin, C. (2014). Open, Flexible and Participatory Pedagogy in the Era of Globalisation: Technology, Open Education and International E-Learning. In V. Wang (Ed.), *International Education and the Next-Generation Workforce: Competition in the Global Economy* (pp. 224–239). Hershey, PA: IGI Global. doi:10.4018/978-1-4666-4498-4.ch013

Mejiuni, O. (2014). Working-Walking Alone and With Others: Working-Walking Fast and Far. In V. Wang (Ed.), *International Education and the Next-Generation Workforce: Competition in the Global Economy* (pp. 240–255). Hershey, PA: IGI Global. doi:10.4018/978-1-4666-4498-4.ch014

Moore, B. (2017). Authentic Leadership: Applications in Academic Decision-Making. In R. Styron Jr & J. Styron (Eds.), *Comprehensive Problem-Solving and Skill Development for Next-Generation Leaders* (pp. 76–94). Hershey, PA: IGI Global. doi:10.4018/978-1-5225-1968-3.ch004

Related Readings

Mukhopadhyay, P. (2017). Investigation of Ergonomic Risk Factors in Snacks Manufacturing in Central India: Ergonomics in Unorganized Sector. In B. Christiansen & H. Chandan (Eds.), *Handbook of Research on Human Factors in Contemporary Workforce Development* (pp. 425–449). Hershey, PA: IGI Global. doi:10.4018/978-1-5225-2568-4.ch019

Munn, S. L. (2016). A Common Methodology: Using Cluster Analysis to Identify Organizational Culture across Two Workforce Datasets. *International Journal of Adult Vocational Education and Technology*, 7(2), 74–87. doi:10.4018/IJAVET.2016040106

Mupepi, M. (2017). A Centricity on Survey Design Techniques: Advancing Talent Management in Emerging Enterprises. In M. Mupepi (Ed.), *Effective Talent Management Strategies for Organizational Success* (pp. 309–319). Hershey, PA: IGI Global. doi:10.4018/978-1-5225-1961-4.ch020

Mupepi, M. (2017). Amplifying the Significance of Systems Theory: Charting the Course in High Velocity Environments. In M. Mupepi (Ed.), *Effective Talent Management Strategies for Organizational Success* (pp. 301–308). Hershey, PA: IGI Global. doi:10.4018/978-1-5225-1961-4.ch019

Mupepi, M. (2017). Diamonds Are Not for Forever: Talent Development at De Beers. In M. Mupepi (Ed.), *Effective Talent Management Strategies for Organizational Success* (pp. 134–159). Hershey, PA: IGI Global. doi:10.4018/978-1-5225-1961-4.ch010

Mupepi, M. (2017). Performance Analysis: Crafting the Flair to Make the Difference. In M. Mupepi (Ed.), *Effective Talent Management Strategies for Organizational Success* (pp. 47–56). Hershey, PA: IGI Global. doi:10.4018/978-1-5225-1961-4.ch004

Mupepi, M. (2017). Single Factor Analysis in Grading Jobs: The How-to Retain Talent. In M. Mupepi (Ed.), *Effective Talent Management Strategies for Organizational Success* (pp. 177–186). Hershey, PA: IGI Global. doi:10.4018/978-1-5225-1961-4.ch012

Mupepi, M., Frey, R., & Motwani, J. (2017). Patents and Logocentric Differences: Protecting the Competitive Advantage. In M. Mupepi (Ed.), *Effective Talent Management Strategies for Organizational Success* (pp. 102–120). Hershey, PA: IGI Global. doi:10.4018/978-1-5225-1961-4.ch008

Mupepi, M., Modak, A., & Frey, R. (2017). Why the Zebra's Stripes are Important: Protecting the Core Competences of the firm. In M. Mupepi (Ed.), *Effective Talent Management Strategies for Organizational Success* (pp. 187–199). Hershey, PA: IGI Global. doi:10.4018/978-1-5225-1961-4.ch013

Mupepi, M., Modak, A., & Mupepi, S. (2017). Shielding the Corporation's Raison d'être: Talent Management in Ubiquitous Value Creation Systems. In M. Mupepi (Ed.), *Effective Talent Management Strategies for Organizational Success* (pp. 121–133). Hershey, PA: IGI Global. doi:10.4018/978-1-5225-1961-4.ch009

Mupepi, M., & Motwani, J. (2017). Deconstructing Talent: Understanding know-how in organization. In M. Mupepi (Ed.), *Effective Talent Management Strategies for Organizational Success* (pp. 83–100). Hershey, PA: IGI Global. doi:10.4018/978-1-5225-1961-4.ch007

Mupepi, M., Motwani, J., Ross-Davis, Y. M., & Allen, M. (2017). Engaging the Diversified Workforce Sustaining Productivity. In M. Mupepi (Ed.), *Effective Talent Management Strategies for Organizational Success* (pp. 201–217). Hershey, PA: IGI Global. doi:10.4018/978-1-5225-1961-4.ch014

Mupepi, M., Mupepi, S., & Modak, A. (2017). Structuration Applications and Practice: Restructuring High Impact Organization. In M. Mupepi (Ed.), *Effective Talent Management Strategies for Organizational Success* (pp. 74–82). Hershey, PA: IGI Global. doi:10.4018/978-1-5225-1961-4.ch006

Mupepi, M., Ross-Davis, Y. M., Davis, M., & Vachon, T. S. (2017). How to Effectively Apply Appreciative Inquiry in Developing Talent in Organizations. In M. Mupepi (Ed.), *Effective Talent Management Strategies for Organizational Success* (pp. 20–30). Hershey, PA: IGI Global. doi:10.4018/978-1-5225-1961-4.ch002

Mupepi, M. G., & Boachie-Mensah, F. (2017). Appreciating Specialization: Nurturing Talent in the Division of Labor. In M. Mupepi (Ed.), *Effective Talent Management Strategies for Organizational Success* (pp. 1–19). Hershey, PA: IGI Global. doi:10.4018/978-1-5225-1961-4.ch001

Mupepi, M. G., & Mupepi, S. C. (2017). The Structure of Talent: A Co-constructed Competency Perspective. In M. Mupepi (Ed.), *Effective Talent Management Strategies for Organizational Success* (pp. 57–73). Hershey, PA: IGI Global. doi:10.4018/978-1-5225-1961-4.ch005

Related Readings

Mupepi, S., Mupepi, M., & Modak, A. (2017). Highly Productive 21st Century Workforce: Tech-Savvy Women in-Charge. In M. Mupepi (Ed.), *Effective Talent Management Strategies for Organizational Success* (pp. 218–234). Hershey, PA: IGI Global. doi:10.4018/978-1-5225-1961-4.ch015

Muralidharan, E., & Pathak, S. (2017). National Ethical Institutions and Social Entrepreneurship. In B. Christiansen & H. Chandan (Eds.), *Handbook of Research on Human Factors in Contemporary Workforce Development* (pp. 379–402). Hershey, PA: IGI Global. doi:10.4018/978-1-5225-2568-4.ch017

Naidoo, V. (2017). E-Learning and Management Education at African Universities. In N. Baporikar (Ed.), *Management Education for Global Leadership* (pp. 181–201). Hershey, PA: IGI Global. doi:10.4018/978-1-5225-1013-0.ch009

Naito, Y. (2017). Factors Related to Readjustment to Daily Life: A Study of Repatriates in Japanese Multinational Enterprises. In B. Christiansen & H. Chandan (Eds.), *Handbook of Research on Human Factors in Contemporary Workforce Development* (pp. 403–424). Hershey, PA: IGI Global. doi:10.4018/978-1-5225-2568-4.ch018

Nayak, S., & Prabhu, N. (2017). Paradigm Shift in Management Education: Need for a Cross Functional Perspective. In N. Baporikar (Ed.), *Management Education for Global Leadership* (pp. 241–255). Hershey, PA: IGI Global. doi:10.4018/978-1-5225-1013-0.ch012

Oppong, N. Y. (2017). Mastering Talent Management: The Uncertainties, Lack of Clarity and Misunderstandings. In M. Mupepi (Ed.), *Effective Talent Management Strategies for Organizational Success* (pp. 31–46). Hershey, PA: IGI Global. doi:10.4018/978-1-5225-1961-4.ch003

Orta, I. M., & Camgoz, S. M. (2017). Exploring Emotional Intelligence at Work: A Review of Current Evidence. In B. Christiansen & H. Chandan (Eds.), *Handbook of Research on Organizational Culture and Diversity in the Modern Workforce* (pp. 346–363). Hershey, PA: IGI Global. doi:10.4018/978-1-5225-2250-8.ch016

Parkar, S. S. (2017). Revamping Pedagogies in Indian B-Schools to Create Global Leaders. In N. Baporikar (Ed.), *Management Education for Global Leadership* (pp. 52–69). Hershey, PA: IGI Global. doi:10.4018/978-1-5225-1013-0.ch003

Patro, C. S. (2017). Performance Appraisal System Effectiveness: A Conceptual Review. In B. Christiansen & H. Chandan (Eds.), *Handbook of Research on Human Factors in Contemporary Workforce Development* (pp. 156–180). Hershey, PA: IGI Global. doi:10.4018/978-1-5225-2568-4.ch007

Patro, C. S. (2017). Welfare Regime: A Critical Discourse. In B. Christiansen & H. Chandan (Eds.), *Handbook of Research on Human Factors in Contemporary Workforce Development* (pp. 110–131). Hershey, PA: IGI Global. doi:10.4018/978-1-5225-2568-4.ch005

Pietiläinen, V., Salmi, I., Rusko, R., & Jänkälä, R. (2017). Experienced Stress and the Value of Rest Stops in the Transportation Field: Stress and Transportation. In B. Christiansen & H. Chandan (Eds.), *Handbook of Research on Human Factors in Contemporary Workforce Development* (pp. 249–267). Hershey, PA: IGI Global. doi:10.4018/978-1-5225-2568-4.ch011

Pulotu-Endemann, F. K., & Faleafa, M. (2017). Developing a Culturally Competent Workforce that Meets the Needs of Pacific People Living in New Zealand. In M. Smith & A. Jury (Eds.), *Workforce Development Theory and Practice in the Mental Health Sector* (pp. 165–180). Hershey, PA: IGI Global. doi:10.4018/978-1-5225-1874-7.ch008

Quellmalz, E. S., Silberglitt, M. D., Buckley, B. C., Loveland, M. T., & Brenner, D. G. (2016). Simulations for Supporting and Assessing Science Literacy. In Y. Rosen, S. Ferrara, & M. Mosharraf (Eds.), *Handbook of Research on Technology Tools for Real-World Skill Development* (pp. 191–229). Hershey, PA: IGI Global. doi:10.4018/978-1-4666-9441-5.ch008

Reio, T. G. Jr, & Whitehead, C. L. (2014). Using Technology to Address Workforce Readiness Skills. In V. Wang (Ed.), *International Education and the Next-Generation Workforce: Competition in the Global Economy* (pp. 154–169). Hershey, PA: IGI Global. doi:10.4018/978-1-4666-4498-4.ch009

Roche, A. M., & Nicholas, R. S. (2017). Mental Health and Addictions Workforce Development: Past, Present, and Future. In M. Smith & A. Jury (Eds.), *Workforce Development Theory and Practice in the Mental Health Sector* (pp. 1–35). Hershey, PA: IGI Global. doi:10.4018/978-1-5225-1874-7.ch001

Related Readings

Rodda, S. N., Abbott, M. W., Dowling, N. A., & Lubman, D. I. (2017). Workforce Development and E-Competency in Mental Health Services. In M. Smith & A. Jury (Eds.), *Workforce Development Theory and Practice in the Mental Health Sector* (pp. 284–301). Hershey, PA: IGI Global. doi:10.4018/978-1-5225-1874-7.ch014

Saini, D. (2017). Relevance of Teaching Values and Ethics in Management Education. In N. Baporikar (Ed.), *Management Education for Global Leadership* (pp. 90–111). Hershey, PA: IGI Global. doi:10.4018/978-1-5225-1013-0.ch005

Saiz-Alvarez, J. M., & Olalla-Caballero, B. (2017). EFQM in Management Education: A Tool for Excellence. In N. Baporikar (Ed.), *Management Education for Global Leadership* (pp. 221–240). Hershey, PA: IGI Global. doi:10.4018/978-1-5225-1013-0.ch011

Salazar, L. R. (2017). Workplace Bullying in Digital Environments: Antecedents, Consequences, Prevention, and Future Directions. In B. Christiansen & H. Chandan (Eds.), *Handbook of Research on Organizational Culture and Diversity in the Modern Workforce* (pp. 132–154). Hershey, PA: IGI Global. doi:10.4018/978-1-5225-2250-8.ch007

Schmidtke, C. (2014). Global Education in the Russian Federation. In V. Wang (Ed.), *International Education and the Next-Generation Workforce: Competition in the Global Economy* (pp. 26–46). Hershey, PA: IGI Global. doi:10.4018/978-1-4666-4498-4.ch002

Schmidtke, C., & Chen, P. (2016). Component Theories for Human Resource Development in China: A Proposition. *International Journal of Adult Vocational Education and Technology*, 7(4), 35–53. doi:10.4018/IJAVET.2016100103

Scott, C. L., & Sims, J. D. (2015). Workforce Diversity Career Development: A Missing Piece of the Curriculum in Academia. In C. Hughes (Ed.), *Impact of Diversity on Organization and Career Development* (pp. 129–150). Hershey, PA: IGI Global. doi:10.4018/978-1-4666-7324-3.ch006

Seino, K., Nomoto, A., Takezawa, T., & Boeltzig-Brown, H. (2017). The Diversity Management for Employment of the Persons With Disabilities: Evidence of Vocational Rehabilitation in the United States and Japan. In B. Christiansen & H. Chandan (Eds.), *Handbook of Research on Human Factors in Contemporary Workforce Development* (pp. 333–356). Hershey, PA: IGI Global. doi:10.4018/978-1-5225-2568-4.ch015

Senaratne, S., & Gunarathne, A. D. (2017). Excellence Perspective for Management Education from a Global Accountants' Hub in Asia. In N. Baporikar (Ed.), *Management Education for Global Leadership* (pp. 158–180). Hershey, PA: IGI Global. doi:10.4018/978-1-5225-1013-0.ch008

Sharma, A. J. (2017). Enhancing Sustainability through Experiential Learning in Management Education. In N. Baporikar (Ed.), *Management Education for Global Leadership* (pp. 256–274). Hershey, PA: IGI Global. doi:10.4018/978-1-5225-1013-0.ch013

Shen, L., & Austin, L. (2017). Communication and Job Satisfaction. In B. Christiansen & H. Chandan (Eds.), *Handbook of Research on Human Factors in Contemporary Workforce Development* (pp. 201–225). Hershey, PA: IGI Global. doi:10.4018/978-1-5225-2568-4.ch009

Sims, C. H. (2015). Genderized Workplace Lookism in the U.S. and Abroad: Implications for Organization and Career Development Professionals. In C. Hughes (Ed.), *Impact of Diversity on Organization and Career Development* (pp. 105–127). Hershey, PA: IGI Global. doi:10.4018/978-1-4666-7324-3.ch005

Singh, R., Chawla, G., & Desai, A. (2017). Job Satisfaction and Teachers Retention: Critical Review of Indian Management Education. In N. Baporikar (Ed.), *Management Education for Global Leadership* (pp. 137–157). Hershey, PA: IGI Global. doi:10.4018/978-1-5225-1013-0.ch007

Smith, M., & Jury, A. F. (2017). Key Initiatives in New Zealand's Adult Mental Health Workforce Development. In M. Smith & A. Jury (Eds.), *Workforce Development Theory and Practice in the Mental Health Sector* (pp. 106–129). Hershey, PA: IGI Global. doi:10.4018/978-1-5225-1874-7.ch005

Related Readings

St George, L. C., O'Hagan, M., Bradstreet, S., & Burge, M. (2017). The Emerging Field of Peer Support within Mental Health Services. In M. Smith & A. Jury (Eds.), *Workforce Development Theory and Practice in the Mental Health Sector* (pp. 222–250). Hershey, PA: IGI Global. doi:10.4018/978-1-5225-1874-7.ch011

Starr-Glass, D. (2017). The Misappropriation of Organizational Power and Control: Managerial Bullying in the Workplace. In B. Christiansen & H. Chandan (Eds.), *Handbook of Research on Human Factors in Contemporary Workforce Development* (pp. 87–109). Hershey, PA: IGI Global. doi:10.4018/978-1-5225-2568-4.ch004

Stein, K. C., & Kim, T. (2017). Teacher Collaborative Inquiry and Democracy in Schools: Possibilities and Challenges. In R. Styron Jr & J. Styron (Eds.), *Comprehensive Problem-Solving and Skill Development for Next-Generation Leaders* (pp. 255–276). Hershey, PA: IGI Global. doi:10.4018/978-1-5225-1968-3.ch012

Storey, V. A., & Richard, B. M. (2014). Europe 2020: Will Higher Education in the European Union be a Catalyst for a More Dynamic, Prosperous Economy? In V. Wang (Ed.), *International Education and the Next-Generation Workforce: Competition in the Global Economy* (pp. 47–63). Hershey, PA: IGI Global. doi:10.4018/978-1-4666-4498-4.ch003

Thompson, K. S. (2017). Training's Impact on Time-to-Proficiency for New Bankers in a Financial Services Organization. In S. Frasard & F. Prasuhn (Eds.), *Training Initiatives and Strategies for the Modern Workforce* (pp. 169–185). Hershey, PA: IGI Global. doi:10.4018/978-1-5225-1808-2.ch009

Thoms, C. L., & Burton, S. L. (2015). Understanding the Impact of Inclusion in Disability Studies Education. In C. Hughes (Ed.), *Impact of Diversity on Organization and Career Development* (pp. 186–213). Hershey, PA: IGI Global. doi:10.4018/978-1-4666-7324-3.ch008

Tiwari, V., & Singh, S. K. (2017). Relationship Among Work-Related Micro-OB Variables: A Model Approach. In B. Christiansen & H. Chandan (Eds.), *Handbook of Research on Organizational Culture and Diversity in the Modern Workforce* (pp. 261–275). Hershey, PA: IGI Global. doi:10.4018/978-1-5225-2250-8.ch012

Tomasiak, M. A., & Chamakiotis, P. (2017). Understanding Diversity in Virtual Work Environments: A Comparative Case Study. In B. Christiansen & H. Chandan (Eds.), *Handbook of Research on Human Factors in Contemporary Workforce Development* (pp. 283–307). Hershey, PA: IGI Global. doi:10.4018/978-1-5225-2568-4.ch013

Tran, B. (2017). Organizational Diversity: From Workforce Diversity to Workplace Inclusion for Persons With Disabilities. In B. Christiansen & H. Chandan (Eds.), *Handbook of Research on Organizational Culture and Diversity in the Modern Workforce* (pp. 100–131). Hershey, PA: IGI Global. doi:10.4018/978-1-5225-2250-8.ch006

Tran, B. (2017). The Art and Science in Communication: Workplace (Cross-Cultural) Communication Skills and Competencies in the Modern Workforce. In B. Christiansen & H. Chandan (Eds.), *Handbook of Research on Human Factors in Contemporary Workforce Development* (pp. 60–86). Hershey, PA: IGI Global. doi:10.4018/978-1-5225-2568-4.ch003

Trinh, M. P. (2015). When Demographic and Personality Diversity are Both at Play: Effects on Team Performance and Implications for Diversity Management Practices. In C. Hughes (Ed.), *Impact of Diversity on Organization and Career Development* (pp. 54–79). Hershey, PA: IGI Global. doi:10.4018/978-1-4666-7324-3.ch003

Uysal, H. T., & Gedik, İ. A. (2017). Effect of Cynical Individual Factor on the Reverse Mobbing Tendency: A Planned Behavior. In B. Christiansen & H. Chandan (Eds.), *Handbook of Research on Organizational Culture and Diversity in the Modern Workforce* (pp. 276–308). Hershey, PA: IGI Global. doi:10.4018/978-1-5225-2250-8.ch013

Vargas-Hernández, J. G. (2017). Professional Integrity in Business Management Education. In N. Baporikar (Ed.), *Management Education for Global Leadership* (pp. 70–89). Hershey, PA: IGI Global. doi:10.4018/978-1-5225-1013-0.ch004

Vavik, L., & Salomon, G. (2016). Twenty First Century Skills vs. Disciplinary Studies? In Y. Rosen, S. Ferrara, & M. Mosharraf (Eds.), *Handbook of Research on Technology Tools for Real-World Skill Development* (pp. 1–12). Hershey, PA: IGI Global. doi:10.4018/978-1-4666-9441-5.ch001

Wang, V. C., Dennett, S. K., & Bryan, V. C. (2014). Chinese Pedagogy or Western Andragogy? In V. Wang (Ed.), *International Education and the Next-Generation Workforce: Competition in the Global Economy* (pp. 1–25). Hershey, PA: IGI Global. doi:10.4018/978-1-4666-4498-4.ch001

Washington, G. D., & Shen, L. (2017). Emotional Intelligence and Job Stress. In B. Christiansen & H. Chandan (Eds.), *Handbook of Research on Human Factors in Contemporary Workforce Development* (pp. 226–248). Hershey, PA: IGI Global. doi:10.4018/978-1-5225-2568-4.ch010

Weisel, L., Patterson, M. B., Becker-Prezocki, M., & Fantine, J. (2017). Align and Redesign: An Evaluative Case Study in Transformation. In S. Frasard & F. Prasuhn (Eds.), *Training Initiatives and Strategies for the Modern Workforce* (pp. 186–224). Hershey, PA: IGI Global. doi:10.4018/978-1-5225-1808-2.ch010

Wittmer, J. L., & Rudolph, C. W. (2015). The Impact of Diversity on Career Transitions over the Life Course. In C. Hughes (Ed.), *Impact of Diversity on Organization and Career Development* (pp. 151–185). Hershey, PA: IGI Global. doi:10.4018/978-1-4666-7324-3.ch007

Yeh Wai Man, H. (2014). An Investigation of the Relationship of Motivation, Attitudes and Environment: Two Hong Kong ESL Learners' Experience. In V. Wang (Ed.), *International Education and the Next-Generation Workforce: Competition in the Global Economy* (pp. 194–207). Hershey, PA: IGI Global. doi:10.4018/978-1-4666-4498-4.ch011

Yıldırım, N., & Korkmaz, Y. (2017). Challenge of Millennials in Project Management: Insights on Attitudes and Perceptions of Generation Y in Software Development Projects. *International Journal of Information Technology Project Management*, 8(2), 87–108. doi:10.4018/IJITPM.2017040106

You, J., Kim, J., & Miller, S. M. (2017). Organizational Learning as a Social Process: A Social Capital and Network Approach. In B. Christiansen & H. Chandan (Eds.), *Handbook of Research on Human Factors in Contemporary Workforce Development* (pp. 132–155). Hershey, PA: IGI Global. doi:10.4018/978-1-5225-2568-4.ch006

About the Authors

Sally Blake is a Professor and Chair of the Education Department at Flagler College in St. Augustine, Florida. Sally has been the PI on more than $600,000 dollars of Eisenhower funds and $700,000 of NASA funds for teacher training and professional development. Sally Blake was the Director and Co-PI of the NSF sponsored Partnership for Excellence in Teacher Education (PETE) and the Noyce Scholarship program at the University of Texas at El Paso, a research fellow with the NSF Center for Research on Educational Reform,(MSP project) a teaching fellow with the NSF Center for Effective Teaching and Learning (MIE project), co-developer of the Research Pedagogical Labs and the MAT degree in the College of Science (MSP project), and Co-PI on the NSF GK-12 grant. She was appointed to The National Summit on Developing a STEM Workforce Strategy at the National Academy of Sciences and the Sesame Street advisory board on the "Words are All Around Us" project.

Candice Burkett is a Doctoral Candidate in the Cognitive Psychology department of the University of Illinois Chicago. She received her Master's degree from the University of Illinois Chicago and her Bachelor's degree from the University of Memphis. Her research interests fall under the broad umbrellas of learning and text comprehension. Specifically, her research is focused on disciplinary literacies, science text comprehension, literary text interpretation, integration of multiple representations and metacognition. She has conducted research on four different highly collaborative grant-funded projects in three labs from two universities. Her research experience is rooted in both empirical laboratory research with undergraduates as well as applied research with students in 6th-12th grade. Candice has been an author on 19 publications and nearly 50 conference presentations and has mentored 15 undergraduate students on research projects. Her undergraduate teaching experience includes: Introduction to Psychology, Research Methods, Statistical Methods in Behavioral Science, Cognitive Psychology and Learning and Motivation.

Index

21st Century 2, 10, 14-17, 25, 49-50, 52, 57, 60, 62

B

Brain 35, 67-72, 76-79, 82-83, 90, 94-96, 111

C

Change 1, 4, 6, 8-9, 12-14, 17, 25, 39, 57, 59, 61-62, 68, 93, 105, 107-110, 112, 116, 123-124
Characteristics of Creative People 38
Cognitive Flexibility 71, 82
Creative People 23-24, 27, 32-35, 38, 48, 56, 67, 91, 96, 100, 108
Creative Potential 8, 61, 90, 92, 98-100
Creative Students 46-47, 49-50, 55-56, 61
Creative Transformation 105, 109, 123
Creativity 1-2, 7-17, 23-38, 46-48, 50-62, 67-69, 71, 73-83, 88, 90-100, 105, 107-110, 112-113, 115-117, 119-124

E

education 1, 3-6, 10, 13-14, 16-17, 27, 32, 46-47, 50-53, 57, 59-61, 68, 91, 98
Educational Environments 32, 48-50, 52-53
Environment 1, 3, 8, 13, 25, 27-29, 32-33, 35, 37-38, 47, 53, 55, 57, 61, 82, 92, 105-113, 115-117, 119, 121-124
Executive Functioning 73, 75-78, 80

Expectations 1-2, 7-8, 29, 32, 46-47, 49, 52, 55-56, 60-61, 92, 107-108, 113, 115-116

I

Importance of Creativity 1-2, 10, 13
Inhibitory Control 67, 78-82, 94
Innovation 1-2, 5, 7-9, 11-15, 17, 23-24, 26, 29-32, 35-39, 46-48, 50-51, 98, 100, 105, 107-109, 112-113, 117, 119, 121, 124
Intelligence 33, 38, 88, 91-96, 105, 124
Intrinsic Motivation 33, 37, 88, 91-92, 94-96, 119-120

M

Misconceptions 23-24, 32, 38
Myths 23-24, 32, 34, 36, 38, 51, 90

N

Neuroscience 68-71

P

Personality 53, 55, 88, 91-96, 112
Prefrontal Cortex 71-73, 75-76, 82, 90, 95

R

Rewards 36, 59, 119-120

S

Support for Creativity 2, 12, 51, 119

W

Workforce 1-9, 11, 16-17, 23-24, 26, 29, 31, 39, 46, 49, 51, 60, 100, 111, 114, 116, 120, 123-124

Workplace 1-3, 5-6, 8, 10, 13, 17, 23-25, 27-32, 36, 38, 47, 58, 82, 88, 95, 105, 107-113, 115-117, 119-124

Workplace Transformation 3, 107, 117

Purchase Print, E-Book, or Print + E-Book

IGI Global books can now be purchased from three unique pricing formats:
Print Only, E-Book Only, or Print + E-Book. Shipping fees apply.

www.igi-global.com

Recommended Reference Books

ISBN: 978-1-4666-8745-5
© 2016; 410 pp.
List Price: $220

ISBN: 978-1-4666-9604-4
© 2016; 378 pp.
List Price: $205

ISBN: 978-1-4666-9624-2
© 2016; 2,266 pp.
List Price: $2,200

ISBN: 978-1-4666-8468-3
© 2015; 1,704 pp.
List Price: $2,395

ISBN: 978-1-4666-9484-2
© 2016; 514 pp.
List Price: $265

ISBN: 978-1-4666-8353-2
© 2015; 438 pp.
List Price: $310

Looking for free content, product updates, news, and special offers?
Join IGI Global's mailing list today and start enjoying exclusive perks sent only to IGI Global members.
Add your name to the list at **www.igi-global.com/newsletters**.

Publishing Information Science and Technology Research Since 1988

IGI Global
DISSEMINATOR of KNOWLEDGE

www.igi-global.com   Sign up at www.igi-global.com/newsletters   facebook.com/igiglobal   twitter.com/igiglobal

Stay Current on the Latest Emerging Research Developments

Become an IGI Global Reviewer for Authored Book Projects

The overall success of an authored book project is dependent on quality and timely reviews.

In this competitive age of scholarly publishing, constructive and timely feedback significantly decreases the turnaround time of manuscripts from submission to acceptance, allowing the publication and discovery of progressive research at a much more expeditious rate. Several IGI Global authored book projects are currently seeking highly qualified experts in the field to fill vacancies on their respective editorial review boards:

Applications may be sent to:
development@igi-global.com

Applicants must have a doctorate (or an equivalent degree) as well as publishing and reviewing experience. Reviewers are asked to write reviews in a timely, collegial, and constructive manner. All reviewers will begin their role on an ad-hoc basis for a period of one year, and upon successful completion of this term can be considered for full editorial review board status, with the potential for a subsequent promotion to Associate Editor.

If you have a colleague that may be interested in this opportunity, we encourage you to share this information with them.

InfoSci®-Books
A Database for Progressive Information Science and Technology Research

www.igi-global.com

Maximize Your Library's Book Collection!

Invest in IGI Global's InfoSci®-Books database and gain access to hundreds of reference books at a fraction of their individual list price.

The InfoSci®-Books database offers unlimited simultaneous users the ability to precisely return search results through more than 75,000 full-text chapters from nearly 3,400 reference books in the following academic research areas:

Business & Management Information Science & Technology • Computer Science & Information Technology
Educational Science & Technology • Engineering Science & Technology • Environmental Science & Technology
Government Science & Technology • Library Information Science & Technology • Media & Communication Science & Technology
Medical, Healthcare & Life Science & Technology • Security & Forensic Science & Technology • Social Sciences & Online Behavior

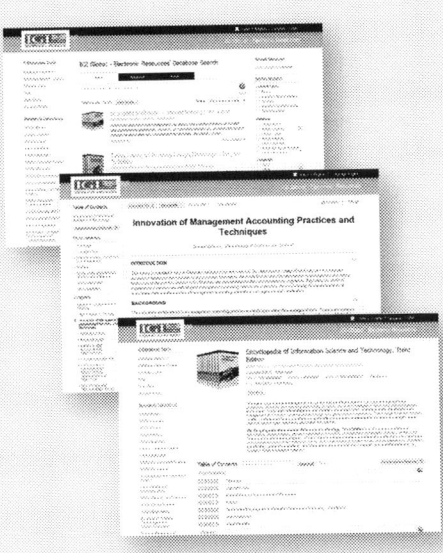

Peer-Reviewed Content:
- Cutting-edge research
- No embargoes
- Scholarly and professional
- Interdisciplinary

Award-Winning Platform:
- Unlimited simultaneous users
- Full-text in XML and PDF
- Advanced search engine
- No DRM

Librarian-Friendly:
- Free MARC records
- Discovery services
- COUNTER4/SUSHI compliant
- Training available

To find out more or request a free trial, visit:
www.igi-global.com/eresources

www.igi-global.com

www.igi-global.com

IGI Global Proudly Partners with

Enhance Your Manuscript with eContent Pro's Professional and Academic **Copy Editing Service**

Additional Services

Expert Translation

eContent Pro Translation provides professional translation services across key languages around the world. Our expert translators will work to provide a clear-cut translation of your document, while maintaining your original meaning and ensuring that your document is accurately and professionally translated.

Professional Proofreading

eContent Pro Proofreading provides fast, high-quality, affordable proofreading that will optimize the accuracy and readability of your document, ensuring that its contents are communicated in the clearest way possible to your readers.

IGI Global Authors Save 20% on eContent Pro's Services!

Scan the QR Code to Receive Your 20% Discount

The 20% discount is applied directly to your eContent Pro shopping cart when placing an order through IGI Global's referral link. Use the QR code to access this referral link. eContent Pro has the right to end or modify any promotion at any time.

Email: customerservice@econtentpro.com

econtentpro.com

Information Resources Management Association

Advancing the Concepts & Practices of Information Resources Management in Modern Organizations

Become an IRMA Member

Members of the **Information Resources Management Association (IRMA)** understand the importance of community within their field of study. The Information Resources Management Association is an ideal venue through which professionals, students, and academicians can convene and share the latest industry innovations and scholarly research that is changing the field of information science and technology. Become a member today and enjoy the benefits of membership as well as the opportunity to collaborate and network with fellow experts in the field.

IRMA Membership Benefits:

- **One FREE Journal Subscription**
- **30% Off Additional Journal Subscriptions**
- **20% Off Book Purchases**
- Updates on the latest events and research on Information Resources Management through the IRMA-L listserv.
- Updates on new open access and downloadable content added to Research IRM.
- A copy of the Information Technology Management Newsletter twice a year.
- A certificate of membership.

IRMA Membership $195

Scan code or visit **irma-international.org** and begin by selecting your free journal subscription.

Membership is good for one full year.

www.irma-international.org

Printed in the United States
By Bookmasters